GOVERNMENT PROCEDURES AND OPERATIONS

TOBACCO PRODUCTS

FDA REGULATION AND USE OF FEES

GOVERNMENT PROCEDURES AND OPERATIONS

Additional books in this series can be found on Nova's website under the Series tab.

Additional e-books in this series can be found on Nova's website under the e-book tab.

GOVERNMENT PROCEDURES AND OPERATIONS

TOBACCO PRODUCTS

FDA REGULATION AND USE OF FEES

JARED HART
EDITOR

New York

For permission to use material from this book please contact us:
Telephone 631-231-7269; Fax 631-231-8175
Web Site: http://www.novapublishers.com

Library of Congress Cataloging-in-Publication Data

ISBN: 978-1-63463-183-9

Published by Nova Science Publishers, Inc. † New York

CONTENTS

PREFACE

This book examines how FDA spent tobacco user fees for key activities using its authorities granted in the act, and any challenges FDA encountered in using its authorities.

Chapter 1 – Tobacco use is the leading cause of preventable death and disease in the United States. In 2009, the Family Smoking Prevention and Tobacco Control Act (Tobacco Control Act) granted FDA, an agency within the Department of Health and Human Services (HHS), authority to regulate tobacco products, including marketing and distribution to youth. The act established CTP, which implements the act by educating the public on the dangers of tobacco use; developing the science needed for tobacco regulation; and developing and enforcing regulations on the manufacture, marketing, and distribution of tobacco products. The act authorized FDA to assess and collect user fees from tobacco manufacturers and importers.

The Tobacco Control Act mandated that GAO review the authority and resources provided to FDA for regulating the manufacture, marketing, and distribution of tobacco products. This report examines (1) how FDA spent tobacco user fees for key activities using its authorities granted in the act, and (2) any challenges FDA encountered in using its authorities. GAO analyzed data on tobacco user fees collected and spent on key activities by FDA as of March 31, 2014; reviewed documents related to FDA's key activities, as well as relevant laws, regulations, and guidance; and interviewed CTP, public health, and tobacco industry officials.

HHS reviewed a draft of this report and agreed with GAO's reiteration of its previous recommendation that performance measures for all tobacco product reviews are needed.

Chapter 2 – On March 19, 2010, the Food and Drug Administration (FDA) reissued a 1996 final rule aimed at reducing underage smoking and use of smokeless tobacco products (e.g., snuff, chewing tobacco). The agency's rulemaking was mandated by the Family Smoking Prevention and Tobacco Control Act, which was enacted last year in response to a 2000 decision by the Supreme Court holding that FDA lacked the statutory authority to regulate tobacco products. The Family Smoking Prevention and Tobacco Control Act (P.L. 111-31) expressly gives FDA broad statutory authority under the Federal Food, Drug, and Cosmetic Act (FFDCA) to regulate the manufacture, distribution, advertising, sale, and use of cigarettes and other tobacco products.

The new FDA tobacco rule builds on the youth access, marketing, and advertising restrictions that the tobacco companies agreed to as part of the 1998 Master Settlement Agreement, which settled lawsuits filed by the states to recover the public health costs of tobacco-related illness. Among its provisions, the rule prohibits the sale of tobacco products to any person under age 18; requires retailers to verify a purchaser's age by photo ID; restricts the sale of tobacco products through vending machines and self-service displays to adult-only facilities; limits tobacco advertising in publications to which children and adolescents are exposed to a black-on-white, text-only format; prohibits the sale of tobacco brand-identified promotional items such as caps and T-shirts; and prohibits brand-name sponsorship of sporting and other cultural events. The rule became effective on June 22, 2010.

The original 1996 rule included a ban on outdoor cigarette and smokeless tobacco advertising (e.g., billboards, posters) within 1,000 feet of schools and playgrounds. The reissued rule does not incorporate such a ban. In *Lorillard Tobacco Co. v. Reilly* (2001), the U.S. Supreme Court struck down a similar outdoor advertising ban in Massachusetts, arguing that it violated the First Amendment protection of commercial speech. FDA has reserved a section in the reissued rule for future rulemaking on outdoor advertising restrictions. In a separate advanced notice of proposed rulemaking, the agency has requested public comment on this issue and offered several options for more narrowly tailored outdoor advertising restrictions that the agency believes would not violate the First Amendment.

In August 2009, several tobacco companies filed a federal lawsuit against FDA claiming that the Family Smoking Prevention and Tobacco Control Act violates their constitutional right to commercial free speech. On March 19, 2012, the U.S. Court of Appeals for the Sixth Circuit upheld the district court's decision striking down the tobacco rule's provision that limits advertising in publications with significant youth readership to a black-on-white, text-only format.

In: Tobacco Products
Editor: Jared Hart

ISBN: 978-1-63463-183-9

Chapter 1

TOBACCO PRODUCT REGULATION: MOST FDA SPENDING FUNDED PUBLIC EDUCATION, REGULATORY SCIENCE, AND COMPLIANCE AND ENFORCEMENT ACTIVITIES*

United States Government Accountability Office

WHY GAO DID THIS STUDY

Tobacco use is the leading cause of preventable death and disease in the United States. In 2009, the Family Smoking Prevention and Tobacco Control Act (Tobacco Control Act) granted FDA, an agency within the Department of Health and Human Services (HHS), authority to regulate tobacco products, including marketing and distribution to youth. The act established CTP, which implements the act by educating the public on the dangers of tobacco use; developing the science needed for tobacco regulation; and developing and enforcing regulations on the manufacture, marketing, and distribution of tobacco products. The act authorized FDA to assess and collect user fees from tobacco manufacturers and importers.

---

* This is an edited, reformatted and augmented version of the United States Government Accountability Office publication, GAO-14-561, dated June 2014.

The Tobacco Control Act mandated that GAO review the authority and resources provided to FDA for regulating the manufacture, marketing, and distribution of tobacco products. This report examines (1) how FDA spent tobacco user fees for key activities using its authorities granted in the act, and (2) any challenges FDA encountered in using its authorities. GAO analyzed data on tobacco user fees collected and spent on key activities by FDA as of March 31, 2014; reviewed documents related to FDA's key activities, as well as relevant laws, regulations, and guidance; and interviewed CTP, public health, and tobacco industry officials.

HHS reviewed a draft of this report and agreed with GAO's reiteration of its previous recommendation that performance measures for all tobacco product reviews are needed.

WHAT GAO FOUND

As of March 31, 2014, the Food and Drug Administration (FDA) spent about $1.48 billion (79 percent) of the $1.88 billion in total tobacco user fees it collected since fiscal year 2009. FDA spent the majority of tobacco user fees on key activities led by the agency's Center for Tobacco Products (CTP), which is funded solely by tobacco user fees. These included activities related to public education (including public education campaigns and communicating CTP activities); regulatory science (including research, product review, and developing the science to support regulations and guidance); and compliance and enforcement (including tobacco retailer inspections; manufacturer and import inspections and enforcement; promotion, advertising, and labeling surveillance; and outreach and small business assistance).

While FDA has taken steps to address some of the challenges it has faced, including challenges related to starting up a new center, it continues to face challenges, including setting and monitoring review time frames. Until recently, CTP has not had performance measures for making final decisions on new tobacco product submissions by which to assess its progress, as GAO previously recommended. FDA has announced performance measures for two of its new tobacco product review processes (to take effect in October 2014), but not for the type of new tobacco product submission that comprises the bulk of FDA's review backlog. The agency has indicated that it intends to establish such performance measures, but until it does so, the agency's ability to assess its efforts will be limited. This will be particularly pressing as FDA moves forward with plans to deem additional types of tobacco products to be subject to its regulatory authority.

ABBREVIATIONS

CDC	Centers for Disease Control and Prevention
CTP	Center for Tobacco Products
FDA	Food and Drug Administration
HHS	Department of Health and Human Services
HPHC	harmful and potentially harmful constituent
MRTP	modified risk tobacco product
NIH	National Institutes of Health
OCE	Office of Compliance and Enforcement
OHCE	Office of Health Communication and Education
ORA	Office of Regulatory Affairs
OS	Office of Science
PMTA	Premarket Tobacco Product Application
SE	Substantial Equivalence

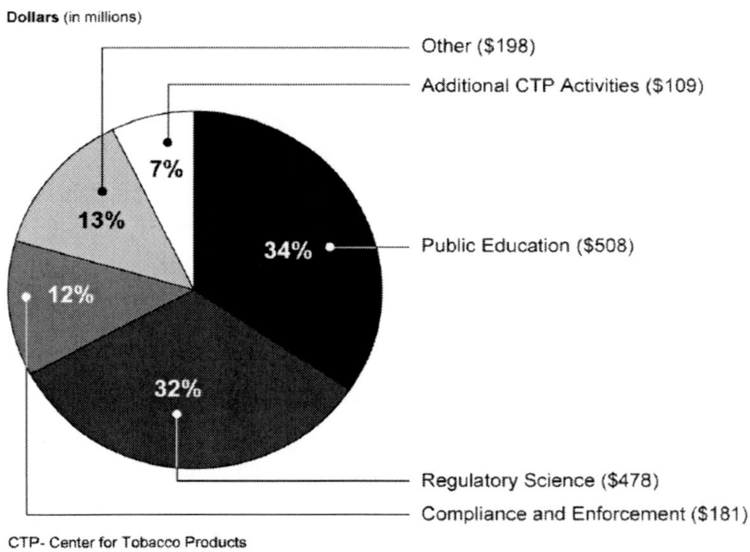

Source: GAO analysis of FDA data | GAO-14-561

Proportion of FDA Tobacco User Fee Spending by Activity as of March 31, 2014.

June 20, 2014

The Honorable Tom Harkin
Chairman
The Honorable Lamar Alexander
Ranking Member
Committee on Health, Education, Labor, and Pensions
United States Senate

The Honorable Fred Upton
Chairman
The Honorable Henry Waxman
Ranking Member
Committee on Energy and Commerce
House of Representatives

Tobacco use is the leading cause of preventable death, disease, and disability and is a significant contributor to health care costs in the United States. Smoking was responsible for more than 480,000 premature deaths annually between 2005 and 2009 among Americans 35 and older, according to the U.S. Surgeon General.[1] The Surgeon General also reported that among adults who had ever smoked cigarettes daily, 87 percent had tried their first cigarette by the time they were 18 years of age. In 2009, the Family Smoking Prevention and Tobacco Control Act (Tobacco Control Act) granted the Food and Drug Administration (FDA), an agency within the Department of Health and Human Services (HHS), authority to address concerns about tobacco use by young people and to regulate the manufacturing, marketing, and distribution of tobacco products using a public health standard.[2] The act provides FDA with a range of authorities, such as restricting tobacco sales to minors and setting tobacco product standards. The Tobacco Control Act represents the first time that FDA has had the authority to regulate tobacco products.

The Tobacco Control Act established the Center for Tobacco Products (CTP) within FDA as the entity responsible for implementing the act.[3] CTP was formed in 2009—the first new center within FDA in 21 years— and it implements the act by educating the public on the dangers of tobacco use; developing the science needed for tobacco regulation; developing and enforcing regulations on the manufacture, marketing, and distribution of tobacco products; and performing other activities. To support FDA's tobacco regulation activities, the Tobacco Control Act authorized FDA to assess and collect user fees—the sole source of funding for CTP's activities— from each tobacco manufacturer and importer subject to FDA's regulation.[4]

The Tobacco Control Act mandated that GAO review FDA's authority and resources to regulate the manufacture, marketing, and distribution of tobacco products.[5] This report examines (1) how FDA spent tobacco user fees for key activities using its authorities granted in the Tobacco Control Act and (2) any challenges FDA encountered in using its authorities granted in the Tobacco Control Act.

To examine how FDA spent tobacco user fees for its key activities using its authorities granted in the Tobacco Control Act, we analyzed data on tobacco user fees collected through March 31, 2014, such as the amounts collected by FDA and the amounts spent by CTP's offices. We also interviewed agency officials and reviewed agency documents, including budget justifications, reports to Congress, performance reports, and agency documentation of CTP's activities to identify the key activities the agency carried out. We analyzed spending data provided by FDA for these activities for fiscal years 2010 through the first half of fiscal year 2014 (March 31, 2014) and planned spending for fiscal year 2014.[6] Spending for key activities included actual spending and an estimated distribution, generated by FDA, of personnel costs across activities within each individual CTP office. For our analysis, we included spending for the tobacco-related work of FDA's Office of Regulatory Affairs (ORA) with CTP's compliance and enforcement activities, since ORA assists CTP by conducting select activities. Other tobacco-related spending by CTP and FDA, including spending on information technology infrastructure and centralized funding for, among other things, furniture, office equipment, and center-wide training; spending for rent and rent-related activities; and the tobacco-related spending of FDA headquarters, including the Office of the Commissioner was not included in our analysis of spending by key activity. We assessed the reliability of FDA data we received by reviewing related documentation, performing data reliability checks (such as examining the data for missing values and checking values against other documentation), and interviewing CTP officials. After taking these steps, we determined that the data we used were sufficiently reliable for our purposes.

To examine any challenges FDA encountered in using its authorities granted in the Tobacco Control Act, including whether FDA faced limitations in its authority to regulate tobacco products, we reviewed relevant laws, tobacco-related regulations and guidance, and the key activities undertaken by FDA to carry out the Tobacco Control Act. We reviewed documents and interviewed agency officials, public health stakeholders, an association representing state and territorial health officials, and tobacco industry stakeholders—including representatives of tobacco manufacturers and tobacco retailers—to obtain information on any challenges FDA encountered, including any challenges associated with limitations in its authorities or resources.

We conducted this performance audit from September 2013 to June 2014 in accordance with generally accepted government auditing standards. Those standards require that we plan and perform the audit to obtain sufficient, appropriate evidence to provide a reasonable basis for our findings and conclusions based on our audit objectives. We believe that the evidence obtained provides a reasonable basis for our findings and conclusions based on our audit objectives.

BACKGROUND

FDA's Authority to Regulate Tobacco Products

The Tobacco Control Act provides FDA with the authority to regulate cigarettes, cigarette tobacco, roll-your-own tobacco, and smokeless tobacco products, as well as the authority to deem other tobacco products to be subject to FDA's regulatory authority.[7] Under the act, FDA has the authority to issue regulations controlling the manufacture, marketing, and distribution of tobacco products. The act also places limitations on FDA's regulatory authority over tobacco products. For example, the Tobacco Control Act prohibits FDA from banning all tobacco products in certain categories, lowering nicotine yields to zero, or raising the minimum age to purchase tobacco.[8] The Tobacco Control Act includes provisions requiring FDA to regulate tobacco products using a public health standard, which takes into account the risks and benefits of tobacco products on both users and non-users of tobacco products. This standard is unique to FDA's regulation of tobacco products, as other products regulated by FDA, such as drugs and medical devices, use a "safe and effective" standard.

FDA executes its regulatory authority under the Tobacco Control Act through CTP. CTP's Office of Health Communication and Education (OHCE), Office of Science (OS), and Office of Compliance and Enforcement (OCE) have primary responsibility for developing the public education, regulatory science, and compliance and enforcement infrastructure for the tobacco program and carrying out the associated activities. CTP has additional offices that support the activities of these offices (see table 1).

Table 1. FDA Center for Tobacco Products (CTP) Offices

Office	Description
Office of the Center Director	• Provides scientific, policy, and managerial leadership and direction to the other offices that constitute the center. • Communicates agency initiatives and guidance to consumers and industry in support of public health.
Office of Compliance and Enforcement	• Advises center officials on compliance and enforcement issues, policies, and procedures relating to regulated tobacco products and industry. • Ensures that regulated tobacco products and the manufacturers, distributors, retailers, and importers of those products are in compliance with the law.
Office of Health Communication and Education	• Leads CTP's public education and communication activities.
Office of Management	• Provides administrative services to support CTP's business operations in the following areas: financial management, information technology, human resources, acquisitions, management analysis, and logistics.
Office of Policy[a]	• Develops and analyzes policy to implement the Tobacco Control Act.
Office of Regulations	• Leads and coordinates the development and issuance of regulatory and policy documents.
Office of Science	• Develops and implements CTP's regulatory science framework and policies in tobacco regulatory development and tobacco product review. • Implements a research agenda to meet regulatory science needs and to evaluate population and public health impact of tobacco products.

Source: GAO summary of FDA information. | GAO-14-561

[a] According to CTP officials, as a result of an organizational review, entities within the Office of Policy were reassigned as of April 1, 2014, to the Office of the Center Director, the Office of Management, and the Office of Science.

In addition to establishing CTP, the Tobacco Control Act required FDA to reissue regulations originally published in 1996 that, among other things, banned cigarette sales to minors.[9] The act also banned all flavors except tobacco and menthol in cigarettes and directed FDA to issue regulations requiring the display of graphic warning labels depicting the negative health consequences of smoking on cigarette packages and advertisements.[10]

The Tobacco Control Act also requires that manufacturers of new tobacco products submit information—for example, a statement of the product's ingredients—to FDA and receive marketing authorization before introducing those new tobacco products into the U.S. market. The act established three pathways for FDA's review of new tobacco product submissions: (1) the Substantial Equivalence (SE) pathway, which is for new tobacco products that have the same characteristics as a predicate tobacco product that is already legally marketed or has different characteristics that do not raise different questions of public health;[11] (2) the Exemption from SE pathway, which is for new tobacco products with minor modification of another product marketed by the same manufacturer;[12] and (3) the Premarket Tobacco Product Application (PMTA) pathway, which is for new tobacco products that do not meet the criteria for the other two pathways.[13] The act also required manufacturers to submit applications to FDA to market modified risk tobacco products (MRTP), which are products that are sold or distributed for use to reduce harm or the risk of tobacco-related disease associated with commercially marketed tobacco products.[14] CTP is responsible for reviewing new tobacco product submissions and MRTP submissions and determining whether manufacturers may introduce the products in those submissions to the U.S. market.

The Tobacco Control Act established several deadlines for FDA activities. For example, the act required FDA to establish, and periodically revise, a list of harmful and potentially harmful constituents (HPHC) by April 1, 2012, and required manufactures to report HPHC data for each regulated tobacco product by April 1, 2013.[15] In addition, FDA was required to publish HPHC information to the public in a format that is understandable and not misleading by April 1, 2013.[16] The Tobacco Control Act also required the Tobacco Products Scientific Advisory Committee—which includes individuals knowledgeable in scientific fields involved in the manufacture, evaluation, or use of tobacco products—to release a report and recommendations about the impact of menthol cigarette use on the public health not later than one year after its establishment.[17]

Tobacco User Fees

The Tobacco Control Act requires FDA to assess user fees on manufacturers and importers of tobacco products that are subject to FDA regulation based on their market share and specifies that tobacco user fees can only be applied toward FDA activities related to the regulation of tobacco products.[18] The total amount of user fees authorized to be collected is specified in the act for each fiscal year, beginning in fiscal year 2009 (see table 2), and the total amount does not vary based on the number of tobacco products under regulation.

Table 2. Total Tobacco User Fee Amounts Authorized by the Tobacco Control Act, Fiscal Years 2009 through 2019

Dollars in millions	
Fiscal year	**User fee amount**
2009	85
2010	235
2011	450
2012	477
2013	505
2014	534
2015	566
2016	599
2017	635
2018	672
2019 and each subsequent year	712

Source: GAO analysis of the Tobacco Control Act. | GAO-14-561

Notes: The amounts shown are the total user fee amounts authorized to be collected by FDA for its regulation of tobacco products. Fees are collected and available for obligation only to the extent and in the amount provided in advance in appropriations acts, with the exception of user fees assessed for fiscal year 2009, which were appropriated by the Tobacco Control Act. All of the Center for Tobacco Products' activities, tobacco-related work of FDA's Office of Regulatory Affairs, other FDA activities related to tobacco regulation (such as work of FDA headquarters and Office of the Commissioner), and other activities such as rent are funded only through tobacco user fees. Because the Tobacco Control Act was enacted during fiscal year 2009, the $85 million authorization for fiscal year 2009 was reduced by a pro-rata amount.

All of CTP's activities—as well as other FDA tobacco-related activities, such as the tobacco-related work of FDA's ORA, which assists CTP with compliance and enforcement activities—are funded through tobacco user fees.[19] User fees are made available to FDA until expended (which means that FDA may carry over user fees to subsequent fiscal years if they are not obligated by the end of the fiscal year in which they were collected). As of March 31, 2014, FDA had collected about $1.88 billion in tobacco user fees.

FDA Spent Nearly 80 Percent of User Fees Collected, Mostly for Public Education, Regulatory Science, and Compliance and Enforcement

FDA spent nearly 80 percent of the tobacco user fees collected as of March 31, 2014, with more than half of its spending occurring in fiscal year 2013. The majority of FDA's spending was for activities related to public education, regulatory science, and compliance and enforcement, with spending for public education and regulatory science activities exceeding spending for compliance and enforcement activities.

FDA Spent 79 Percent of User Fees Collected, Mostly in Fiscal Year 2013

As of March 31, 2014, FDA spent about $1.48 billion (79 percent) of the $1.88 billion in tobacco user fees collected (see Figure 1).[20] More than half of FDA's spending—$868 million—occurred in fiscal year 2013.

FDA spending for tobacco-related activities increased over time, from about $67 million in fiscal year 2010 to about $868 million in fiscal year 2013 (see Figure 2).[21] Between fiscal years 2012 and 2013, FDA spending nearly tripled. In fiscal year 2014, FDA spent $98 million as of March 31, 2014, out of the $608 million the agency plans to spend for the fiscal year.[22]

We previously reported that, as of fiscal year 2012, more than half of tobacco user fees collected were unspent and remained available for obligation as FDA, particularly OHCE, did not spend as planned in fiscal years 2011 and 2012.[23] For example, in fiscal year 2012, OHCE planned to spend over $264 million, but it spent less than $34 million that year. According to FDA, issues related to contracting accounted for most of the difference between the amounts actually spent and planned spending. As these issues were addressed, FDA carried out a number of activities in fiscal year 2013 that were originally planned for fiscal years 2011 and 2012. (For more information on the activities carried out by each of CTP's offices, and the spending on those activities, see app. I.)

Most Spending Was for Public Education, Regulatory Science, and Compliance and Enforcement Activities

About 79 percent ($1.17 billion) of user fees spent as of March 31, 2014, on tobacco-related activities was for activities related to public education, regulatory science—which includes product research, product review, and regulation and guidance support—and compliance and enforcement. These activities were carried out by OHCE, OS, and OCE, respectively. Most of the spending was for public education and regulatory science activities, with nearly all of the public education spending occurring in fiscal year 2013. (See Figure 3.)

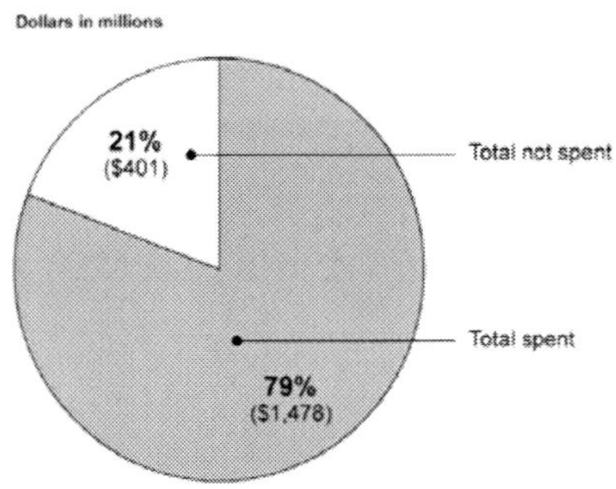

Source: GAO analysis of FDA data | GAO-14-561

Notes: This figure shows the tobacco user fees collected from fiscal year 2009 through the first half of fiscal year 2014 (which totaled about $1.88 billion), the percentage and amount of these fees spent during this period, and the percentage and amount of these fees remaining unspent at the end of this period. Of the $1.48 billion spent by FDA, the Center for Tobacco Products and Office of Regulatory Affairs spent about $1.42 billion. The remaining funds were spent by other FDA entities (including headquarters and the Office of the Commissioner) and spent on U.S. General Services Administration rent, other rent, and rent-related activities.

Figure 1. Total Tobacco User Fees Spent and Not Spent by FDA as of March 31, 2014.

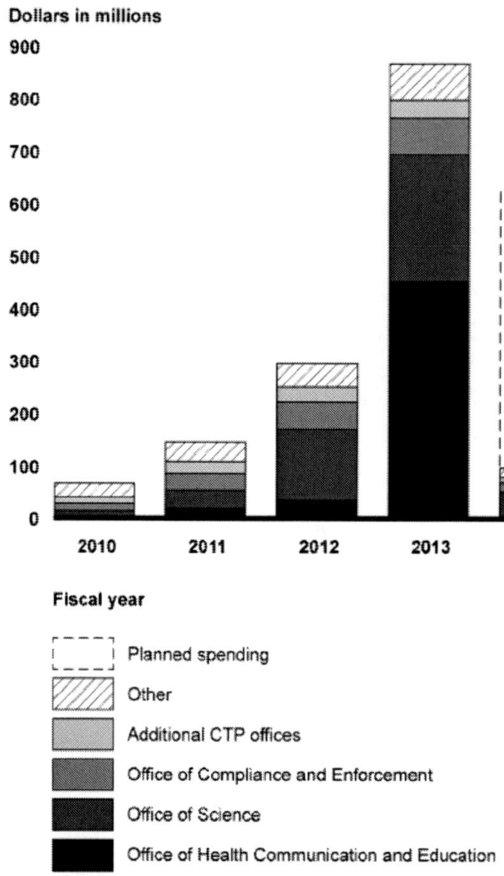

Source: GAO analysis of FDA data | GAO-14-561

Notes: Figure excludes $4.9 million spent by CTP for startup activities in fiscal year 2009.

Other includes CTP overhead (information technology infrastructure and centralized funding for, among other things, furniture, office equipment, and center-wide training); the tobacco-related spending of FDA headquarters and the Office of the Commissioner; and U.S. General Services Administration rent, other rent, and rent-related activities.

Additional CTP offices include CTP's Office of the Center Director, Office of Management, Office of Policy, and Office of Regulations.

Office of Compliance and Enforcement includes spending for FDA's Office of Regulatory Affairs' tobacco-related activities.

Figure 2. FDA Spending by Center for Tobacco Products (CTP) Office as of March 31, 2014.

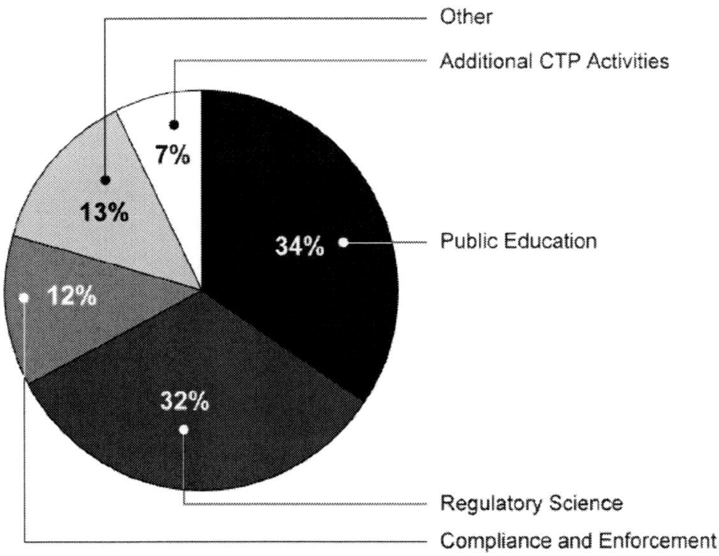

Actual dollars (in millions):
Public Education- $508
Regulatory Science- $478
Compliance and Enforcement- $181
Other- $198
Additional CTP Activities- $109

CTP- Center for Tobacco Products

Source: GAO analysis of FDA data | GAO-14-561

Notes: Figure excludes $4.9 million spent by CTP for startup activities in fiscal year 2009.

Other includes CTP overhead (information technology infrastructure and centralized funding for, among other things, furniture, office equipment, and center-wide training); the tobacco-related spending of FDA headquarters and the Office of the Commissioner; and U.S. General Services Administration rent, other rent, and rent-related activities.

Additional CTP activities include those carried out by CTP's Office of the Center Director, Office of Management, Office of Policy, and Office of Regulations.

Regulatory science includes tobacco product research, product review, and regulation and guidance support activities.

Spending for compliance and enforcement activities includes tobacco-related spending of FDA's Office of Regulatory Affairs.

Percentages do not add to 100 percent due to rounding.

Figure 3. Proportion of FDA Tobacco User Fee Spending by Activity as of March 31, 2014.

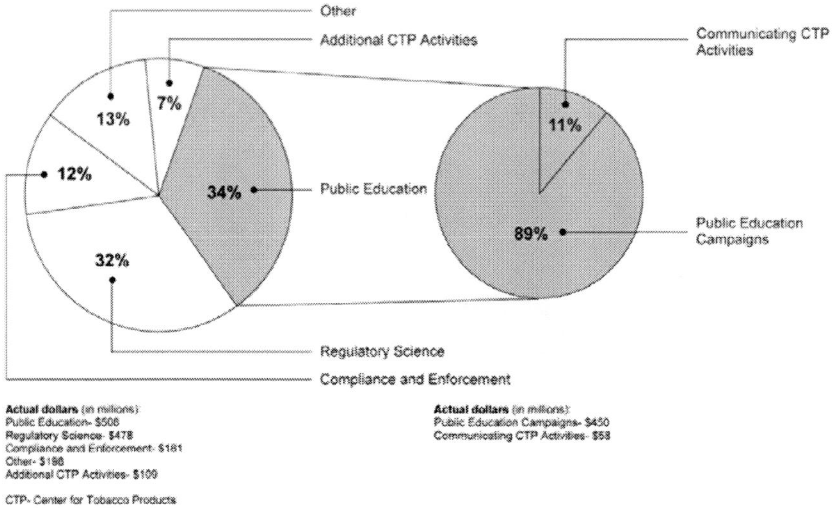

Source: GAO analysis of FDA data | GAO-14-561

Notes: Figure excludes $4.9 million spent by CTP for startup activities in fiscal year 2009.

Other includes CTP overhead (information technology infrastructure and centralized funding for, among other things, furniture, office equipment, and center-wide training); the tobacco-related spending of FDA headquarters and the Office of the Commissioner; and U.S. General Services Administration rent, other rent, and rent-related activities.

Additional CTP activities include those carried out by CTP's Office of the Center Director, Office of Management, Office of Policy, and Office of Regulations.

Regulatory science includes tobacco product research, product review, and regulation and guidance support activities.

Spending for compliance and enforcement activities includes tobacco-related spending of FDA's Office of Regulatory Affairs.

Percentages do not add to 100 percent due to rounding.

Figure 4. Proportion of FDA Tobacco User Fee Spending on Public Education Activities as of March 31, 2014.

Public Education Activities

Spending for FDA's public education activities has focused on (1) developing and launching public education campaigns to educate consumers, particularly youth, on the dangers of tobacco use and (2) communicating information on CTP activities to the public. As of March 31, 2014, 89 percent ($450 million) of the $508 million FDA spent on tobacco public education activities went to develop and launch public education campaigns (see Figure

4). Almost all of this spending ($430 million) occurred in fiscal year 2013, when FDA awarded task orders for its public education campaigns.

Public Education Campaigns

In February 2014, FDA launched its first youth tobacco prevention public education campaign, targeting at-risk youth. FDA plans to launch four additional campaigns targeted at rural; multicultural; lesbian, gay, bisexual, and transgender; and American Indian/Alaska Native youth in fiscal years 2015 and 2016. According to CTP officials, CTP has been working with contractors to develop research plans and create campaign materials for its media campaigns. The task orders for the 5 youth public education campaigns—which were awarded in fiscal year 2013 after the agency spent about 2 years developing an acquisitions infrastructure—account for nearly $314 million of the $450 million spent on public education campaign efforts since fiscal year 2010. According to FDA, the agency focused its public education campaigns on youth prevention because tobacco use is almost always initiated and established during adolescence. The goal of the public education campaigns is to reduce the number of youth who experiment with tobacco use to ultimately reduce the number of future tobacco users.[24]

FDA's first public education campaign, "The Real Cost" campaign, targets youth from ages 12 to 17 who are open to smoking or already experimenting with cigarettes. The campaign launched nationally in a variety of media outlets, including online, and is expected to run for at least 1 year. Campaign messages are intended to make the target audience aware of the risks of smoking by highlighting consequences that, according to FDA, concern youth, such as loss of control due to addiction and health effects like tooth loss and skin damage.[25] Additionally, the campaign will include messages that specifically address the health consequences of menthol cigarettes.

FDA also awarded an evaluation contract in an effort to determine the impact of its youth public education campaigns. Baseline evaluation began in fiscal year 2014, prior to the launch of the first campaign. According to CTP officials, additional evaluations will be conducted at various intervals appropriate for each of the campaigns and evaluation results will be used to assess changes in key tobacco-related knowledge, attitudes, beliefs, and behaviors over several years to determine if exposure to the campaigns is associated with a decrease in cigarette smoking among youth.[26]

In addition to its youth-targeted public education campaigns, FDA has funded two additional public education campaigns, one targeting consumers at the point-of-sale and one for retailer education. Point-of-sale campaign materials target adults who are social smokers and adult smokers who are ready to quit. FDA's "Break the Chain of Tobacco Addiction" campaign was developed by CTP in fiscal year 2010 and provides retailer education designed to encourage voluntary compliance with all FDA regulations. Task orders for these campaigns totaled an additional $84 million of the $450 million spent on public education media campaigns since fiscal year 2010. Like FDA's youth-targeted campaigns, FDA officials stated that the agency plans to evaluate these campaigns to determine their impact.

Communicating CTP Activities

According to FDA officials, the agency's other public education activities involve communicating CTP's mission and regulatory activities to stakeholders—including tobacco manufacturers, retailers, public health stakeholders, and lawmakers, among others—and the public. FDA issues press releases and conducts media outreach, such as outreach to publicize tobacco regulations and the results of CTP's compliance and enforcement work; develops and maintains CTP's website; develops written materials such as frequently-asked questions and materials for CTP events; and assists the individual offices with written communications. In addition, FDA holds webinars to improve education and dissemination of information to stakeholders and listening sessions to provide stakeholders with the opportunity to make comments and raise concerns.

Regulatory Science Activities

FDA spending related to regulatory science has focused on three activities: (1) building a scientific research base, including research on tobacco products and use patterns, (2) developing and implementing a tobacco product review process, and (3) developing the scientific basis to support regulations and guidance. As of March 31, 2014, about 94 percent of the $478 million FDA had spent on regulatory science activities went to building a scientific research base on tobacco products and tobacco use, including spending for a longitudinal study and centers for tobacco regulatory science (see Figure 5). The proportion of spending on regulatory science activities that has been dedicated to building the scientific research base has remained fairly consistent since fiscal year 2010.[27]

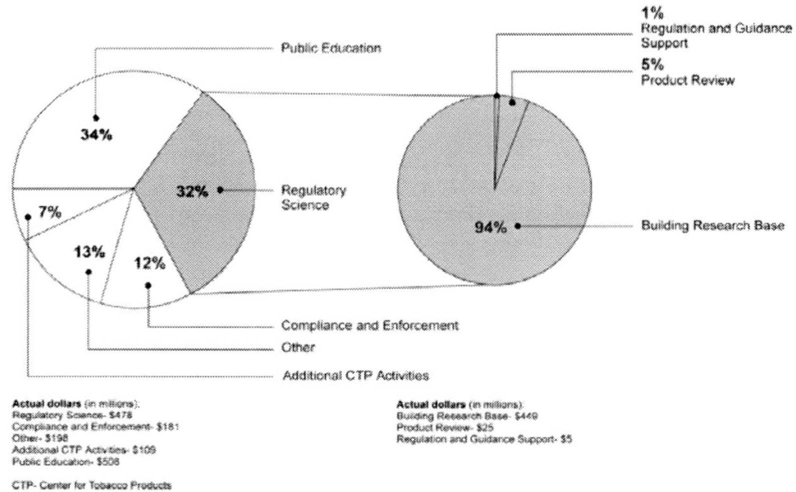

Source: GAO analysis of FDA data | GAO-14-561

Notes: Figure excludes $4.9 million spent by CTP for startup activities in fiscal year 2009.

Other includes CTP overhead (information technology infrastructure and centralized funding for, among other things, furniture, office equipment, and center-wide training); the tobacco-related spending of FDA headquarters and the Office of the Commissioner; and U.S. General Services Administration rent, other rent, and rent-related activities.

Additional CTP activities include those carried out by CTP's Office of the Center Director, Office of Management, Office of Policy, and Office of Regulations.

Regulatory science includes tobacco product research, product review, and regulation and guidance support activities.

Spending for compliance and enforcement activities includes tobacco-related spending of FDA's Office of Regulatory Affairs.

Percentages do not add to 100 percent due to rounding.

Figure 5. Proportion of FDA Tobacco User Fee Spending on Regulatory Science Activities as of March 31, 2014.

Table 3. FDA Spending on Tobacco-Related Research Projects as of March 31, 2014

Dollars in thousands					
FDA spending on research conducted or overseen by FDA or other entities (number of projects)					
Fiscal year	**FDA[a]**	**National Institutes of Health**	**Centers for Disease Control and Prevention**	**Non-federal entities[b]**	**Total**
2010	$0 (0)	$529 (3)	$5 (3)	$4,135 (4)	**$4,669(10)**
2011	322 (3)	10,413 (3)	14,551 (10)	1,947 (5)	**27,233(21)**
2012	6,874(7)	63,237 (43)	32,923 (15)	3,344(10)	**106,378(75)**
2013	10,541(10)	177,104 (94)	27,554 (15)	4,842 (15)	**220,041(134)**
2014[c]	2,840(13)	9,175(10)	21,237(9)	6,123 (8)	**39,375(40)**
Total	**$20,577(33)**	**$260,458(153)**	**$96,270 (52)**	**$20,391(42)**	**$397,696 (280)**

Source: GAO analysis of FDA information. | GAO-14-561

Notes: This table presents the research projects completed or in progress (as of March 31, 2014). The agencies and non-federal entities listed either conducted or had oversight over the tobacco user-fee funded projects.

[a] FDA's research is conducted by its National Center for Toxicological Research.

[b] Non-federal entities include, for example, the Research Triangle Institute International, American Association of Poison Control Centers, American College of Cardiology, and Battelle Memorial Institute.

[c] Spending is for the first two quarters of fiscal year 2014.

Building a Scientific Research Base

Since fiscal year 2010, FDA has funded scientific research to better understand tobacco products, their impact on the health of users and non-users, use patterns and perceptions of tobacco products, and the effectiveness of tobacco marketing, advertising, and graphic warning labels.[28] These research projects, funded by FDA tobacco user fees, have been conducted in collaboration with other federal entities, such as the National Institutes of Health (NIH) and Centers for Disease Control and Prevention (CDC), as well as with non-federal entities (see table 3).

FDA initiated some key long-term projects to help build its scientific research base. For example, FDA funded a 5-year contract in fiscal year 2011 in collaboration with NIH to conduct the Population Assessment of Tobacco and Health study through an NIH contract. The study is a national longitudinal study of tobacco use and how it affects the population's health.[29] The study's objectives include examining reasons why some people use tobacco and others do not, and how and why people start using different tobacco products. According to FDA, study findings will provide a scientific framework to inform decisions about tobacco products and future changes in tobacco products.[30] FDA spent $113 million on the study in fiscal year 2011 through March 31, 2014. FDA, in collaboration with NIH, also awarded $53 million in grants in fiscal year 2013 to fund 14 Tobacco Centers of Regulatory Science to generate public health research to inform tobacco regulation and to train tobacco regulatory scientists.[31] The Tobacco Centers of Regulatory Science funded research including a project focused on understanding the cardiovascular effects of tobacco use to determine the specific elements of tobacco products contributing to cardiovascular injury, which could ultimately help inform regulatory standards for tobacco products. FDA expects to spend more than $273 million in funding for these research projects through fiscal year 2018.

In addition to funding research projects to better understand tobacco products already under FDA's regulatory authority, in fiscal year 2013, FDA also funded scientific research related to tobacco products not yet under the agency's authority, including research projects on e-cigarettes and cigars.[32] For example, in order to inform CTP's regulatory efforts, the agency funded research examining consumer perceptions, attitudes, and beliefs about new and emerging products, such as e-cigarettes and little cigars. According to CTP officials, this research will help inform decisions on how to regulate these other tobacco products. (See app. II for additional examples of research projects supported by FDA spending.)

Developing and Implementing a Tobacco Product Review Process

FDA's regulatory science activities also included establishing and implementing processes for reviewing submissions made by manufacturers to market new tobacco products and submissions for marketing MRTPs, and for receiving and assessing adverse event and product problem reports. FDA receives submissions for CTP to review and determine whether manufacturers may introduce new tobacco products to the U.S. market or market MRTPs. CTP developed and implemented the review processes for such submissions, which FDA began receiving in June 2010 and were mostly submitted through the SE pathway.[33]

FDA made its first decisions on SE submissions in late June 2013—about 3 years after FDA's receipt of the first SE submission. As of March 31, 2014, FDA had made a final decision on a total of 30 regular SE submissions,[34] finding 17 submissions to be substantially equivalent and 13 submissions to be not substantially equivalent to a predicate tobacco product.[35] FDA had made a final decision on a total of four provisional SE submissions,[36] finding all of them to be not substantially equivalent to a predicate and requiring the products to be removed from the market. (See table 4).[37] CTP officials reported that CTP prioritized regular SE submissions over provisional SE submissions because tobacco products in provisional SE submissions can remain on the market legally unless and until FDA issues an order of not substantially equivalent whereas products in regular SE submissions cannot enter the market until FDA issues an order that it is substantially equivalent to a predicate.[38]

In addition to conducting reviews of submissions, FDA designed and implemented a system in fiscal year 2013 to receive and assess tobacco product adverse event and product problem reports to inform the agency's regulation of tobacco products. The reports are submitted by tobacco product consumers and healthcare professionals using the FDA/NIH Safety Reporting Portal.[39] CTP's OS has been systematically assessing the adverse events, product quality problems, and product use errors included in the reports to inform FDA regulation of tobacco product development, manufacture, and marketing. According to CTP officials, the ongoing assessment of the reports is critical to identifying and understanding risks, especially as the tobacco industry develops novel products in response to market and regulatory influences. For example, the assessment of adverse events reported by a large and diverse population of consumers may reveal problems that were not anticipated while the product was being used in research studies.

Regulation and Guidance Support

FDA's regulatory science activities also include developing the scientific basis to support regulations and guidance for the tobacco industry, including proposed regulations to deem additional tobacco products to be subject to FDA's authority and guidance on reporting and submission review. According to FDA officials, from fiscal years 2010 through 2013, much of FDA's initial work to develop tobacco regulations and guidance focused on activities related to requirements in the Tobacco Control Act, including activities to develop regulations on menthol flavoring in cigarettes and guidance for industry's reporting of HPHCs in regulated tobacco products.

FDA has evaluated the science of menthol in cigarettes to determine what action, if any, the agency will take to regulate menthol. In March 2011, FDA received the Tobacco Products Scientific Advisory Committee report on menthol in cigarettes, which found that the removal of menthol cigarettes from the marketplace would benefit public health in the United States.[40] Following the report, FDA conducted an additional, independent evaluation on the effects of menthol in cigarettes, which resulted in similar conclusions.[41] On July 24, 2013, FDA issued an Advanced Notice of Proposed Rule Making to obtain comments or other information that may inform the regulatory actions FDA might take with respect to menthol in cigarettes.[42] According to CTP officials, FDA is reviewing the responses to the notice.

FDA also worked on developing guidance for HPHCs. In August 2011, FDA issued a public notice listing 96 HPHCs in tobacco products and tobacco smoke that research indicated were harmful or potentially harmful to health. Based on public comment and FDA's review of the scientific literature, FDA published a list of 93 HPHCs in April 2012.[43] Also, in March 2012, FDA issued draft guidance for industry on reporting on these HPHCs.[44] FDA also conducted research required by the Tobacco Control Act to ensure it publishes a list of HPHCs that will not be misleading to the public.[45] Based on this research, the Tobacco Products Scientific Advisory Committee and FDA's Risk Communication Advisory Committee made recommendations on further research and strategies FDA might use to effectively communicate the HPHC information to the public. Although FDA planned to publish a proposed regulation to implement the Tobacco Control Act requirements related to the testing and reporting of HPHCs by December 2013, it has not done so.[46]

Table 4. Status of FDA Review of Submissions Made Under Pathways to Market New Tobacco Products and Submissions for Modified Risk Tobacco Products (MRTP) as of March 31, 2014

					Decisions			
Submission type		**Submissions received**	**Initial review completed**[a]	**Closed review without decision (withdrawn by manufacturer)**	**Product meets criteria for marketing**	**Product does *not* meet criteria for marketing**	**Refuse to accept or refuse to file**[b]	**Review pending**
Substantial Equivalence (SE) pathway[c]	Provisional[d]	3,564	3,231	133	0	4	0	3,427
	Regular[e]	981	739	201	17	13	0	750
	Total SE	4,545	3,970	334	17	17	0	4,177
Exemption from SE pathway[f]		61	23	0	0	0	36	25
Premarket Tobacco Product Application (PMTA) pathway[g]		4	0	0	0	0	4	0
MRTP[h]		7	0	1	0	0	6	0

Source: GAO summary of FDA information. | GAO-14-561

Notes: The Tobacco Control Act also requires that manufacturers of new tobacco products submit information—for example, a statement of the product's ingredients—to FDA and receive marketing authorization before introducing those new tobacco products into the U.S. market.

[a] The reviews for submissions represented in this column were pending as of March 31, 2014—that is, they were not withdrawn by manufacturers and FDA had not reached a final decision. Initial review steps include the Center for Tobacco Products' (CTP) determination of whether the new product is a type regulated by FDA and whether the submission is missing information.

[b] FDA may refuse to accept or refuse to file a submission if the submission is missing certain information, such as a full statement of the components, ingredients, additives, and properties of the tobacco product that is the subject of the submission.

[c] Manufacturers use the SE pathway if a new tobacco product has the same characteristics as a predicate tobacco product (a product commercially marketed in the United States on February 15, 2007, or previously found by FDA to be substantially equivalent); or has different characteristics, but does not raise different questions of public health.

[d] Provisional SE submissions are for new tobacco products commercially marketed after February 15, 2007, but before March 22, 2011. Provisional SE submissions were received by FDA by March 22, 2011. The tobacco products represented in these submissions may be commercially marketed unless and until CTP issues an order that they are not substantially equivalent.

[e] Regular SE submissions are for new tobacco products not yet commercially marketed. Regular SE submissions were received by FDA after March 22, 2011. The tobacco products represented in these submissions may not be marketed until CTP issues an order that they are substantially equivalent.

[f] Manufacturers use the Exemption from SE pathway for new tobacco products if the product is modified by adding, deleting, or changing the quantity of an additive and the modification would be a minor modification of another product marketed by the same manufacturer.

[g] Manufacturers use the PMTA pathway for new tobacco products that do not meet the criteria for the SE or Exemption from SE pathways. Products included in PMTA submissions may only be legally marketed after FDA issues an order permitting their marketing. According to CTP officials and industry representatives, one reason for the lack of submissions under the PMTA pathway may be the challenge in demonstrating that a manufacturer has met the public health standard (appropriate for the protection of the public health) to obtain approval under the PMTA pathway.

[h] Manufacturers submit applications to FDA to market MRTP products, which are products that are sold or distributed for use to reduce harm or the risk of tobacco-related disease associated with commercially marketed tobacco products. Manufacturers must submit data from studies on the health risks associated with the MRTP in comparison to the health risks of other products on the market, the MRTP's effect on the likelihood that current tobacco users will stop using tobacco products, and the likelihood that persons who do not use tobacco products will start using the MRTP.

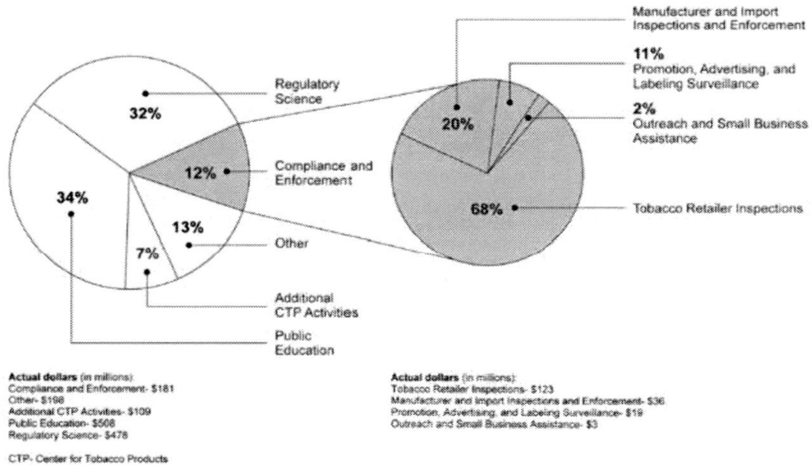

Source: GAO analysis of FDA information. | GAO-14-561

Notes: Figure excludes $4.9 million spent by CTP for startup activities in fiscal year 2009.

Other includes CTP overhead (information technology infrastructure and centralized funding for, among other things, furniture, office equipment, and center-wide training); the tobacco-related spending of FDA headquarters and the Office of the Commissioner; and U.S. General Services Administration rent, other rent, and rent-related activities.

Additional CTP activities include those carried out by CTP's Office of the Center Director, Office of Management, Office of Policy, and Office of Regulations.

Regulatory science includes tobacco product research, product review, and regulation and guidance support activities.

Spending for compliance and enforcement activities includes tobacco-related spending of FDA's Office of Regulatory Affairs.

Percentages do not add to 100 percent due to rounding.

Figure 6. Proportion of FDA Tobacco User Fee Spending on Compliance and Enforcement Activities as of March 31, 2014.

FDA also issued guidance for industry on other topics, including the recommended components of product review submissions and the product review process. For example, in January 2011—about 2 months prior to the statutory deadline for submitting provisional SE submissions—FDA issued a guidance document for tobacco manufacturers to use for making SE submissions,[47] and in September 2011 FDA issued a draft guidance document with responses to frequently asked questions for SE submissions.[48] According to CTP officials, in fiscal year 2014, FDA plans to issue final guidance on frequently asked questions for SE submissions and draft guidance for investigational tobacco products.

Compliance and Enforcement Activities

FDA's tobacco compliance and enforcement activities have been focused on (1) tobacco retailer inspections; (2) inspections and enforcement of domestic manufacturers and imported tobacco products, and determinations of eligible predicate products in SE submissions; (3) surveillance and review of tobacco promotions, advertising, and labeling; and (4) outreach and small business assistance. As of March 31, 2014, about 68 percent of the $181 million FDA spent on compliance and enforcement activities was for tobacco retailer inspection activities (see Figure 6), which has accounted for the majority of compliance and enforcement spending each year since fiscal year 2010.

Tobacco Retailer Inspections

To help ensure that U.S. retailers are in compliance with tobacco laws and regulations, FDA began awarding contracts to states and territories in fiscal year 2010 to implement its tobacco retailer inspection program.[49] As of March 31, 2014, FDA had awarded over $91 million in contracts for retail inspections.

Tobacco retailer inspections, according to FDA officials, include undercover purchases to determine if retailers are selling to minors or are engaging in other practices prohibited under the Tobacco Control Act and its implementing regulations, such as the restriction on sales through vending machines and the ban on cigarettes with certain characterizing flavors, such as grape, coconut, and chocolate. If violations are identified, FDA may issue a warning letter or take enforcement action, such as assessing civil monetary penalties or imposing no-tobacco-sale orders.[50] Warning letters are the agency's principal means of notifying retailers of a first time violation and are used to encourage prompt voluntary compliance. If subsequent violations are found during re-inspection, FDA may initiate administrative action that can result in the imposition of a fine, or civil monetary penalty, based on the number of violations and period of time within which they occurred. For example, at one retailer that had already received a warning letter for a violation, inspectors found two additional violations less than a year later—for selling tobacco products to minors and failing to verify the age of a person purchasing tobacco products. As a result, FDA assessed a civil monetary penalty against this retailer for three violations within a 24-month period.

As of March 31, 2014, 45 states and territories were under contract with FDA to conduct retailer compliance inspections—a threefold increase over the number at the end of fiscal year 2010 (see table 5).[51] As of March 31, 2014, over 279,000 retailer compliance inspections had been conducted, resulting in issuance of more than 14,000 warning letters and 1,347 civil monetary penalties. While FDA plans to contract with additional states and territories in fiscal year 2014, according to FDA officials, the agency is in the process of contracting with third parties, including private entities, to facilitate inspections in those states and territories not currently under contract. According to FDA, it awarded one new contract to a private contractor in April 2014 to facilitate retailer inspections in Florida and two additional third-party contracts in May 2014 to facilitate retailer inspections in North Dakota and South Dakota. CTP officials said that in addition to third-parties, CTP has its own inspectors on staff to inspect in states not currently under contract with FDA. As of March 31, 2014, the office has completed more than half of the planned 100,000 retailer inspections for fiscal year 2014.

In addition to awarding contracts, FDA developed training programs for state and territorial inspection officials to ensure inspections are performed in accordance with FDA requirements. Specifically, according to CTP officials, CTP's OCE is responsible for providing technical support through periodic conference calls with inspection program coordinators, conducting annual in-person training regarding changes to the program, and requiring annual refresher training for inspectors. As of March 31, 2014, OCE reported training inspectors in all states and territories awarded contracts for retailer inspections, with more than 1,000 program coordinators and inspectors trained in fiscal year 2013. The office also developed a system for collecting and tracking information during inspections called the Tobacco Inspection Management System. According to OCE officials, inspectors use their mobile devices to upload data into the system, which is subsequently reviewed by OCE for potential violations. When appropriate, OCE issues enforcement actions.

Manufacturer and Import Inspections and Enforcement

FDA conducts inspections of registered domestic manufacturing facilities, oversees imported tobacco, and determines the status of the predicate product cited in SE submissions.[52] Beginning in fiscal year 2012, FDA has conducted biennial inspections of tobacco manufacturing facilities—FDA's ORA conducts these inspections with the support of OCE as subject matter experts. According to FDA, the agency inspects manufacturing facilities for compliance with Tobacco Control Act requirements, including product and ingredient listing; packaging, labeling, and advertising requirements; and marketing authorization for new or modified risk tobacco products.[53] As of March 31, 2014, FDA conducted 116 inspections at 100 registered manufacturing facilities.[54] According to FDA officials, no warning letters have been issued or other enforcement actions taken as a result of manufacturer inspections.

FDA also implemented an import compliance program for tobacco products beginning in fiscal year 2012.[55] According to FDA officials, ORA and U.S. Customs and Border Protection review imported tobacco products, conduct field exams, and maintain import bulletins and alerts that identify tobacco products in violation of the Tobacco Control Act. Any tobacco product found to violate regulatory requirements may be refused entry into the United States. For example, imported tobacco products that are labeled or advertised as "light," "mild," or "low," and cigarettes that are labeled as having certain characterizing flavors other than tobacco and menthol, such as strawberry, grape, and vanilla, may be detained. As of March 31, 2014, FDA published four import alerts, including one for flavored cigarettes; one for regulated tobacco products using "light," "mild," or "low" in advertising or labeling; one for smokeless tobacco products without the required warning label; and one for tobacco products found to be not substantially equivalent—and refused the entry of two tobacco product imports.

OCE also assists OS in the tobacco product review process by determining if the tobacco product to which the new tobacco product is being compared in an SE submission meets the statutory requirements for a predicate tobacco product. In fiscal years 2011 through 2013, OCE completed over 1,350 predicate eligibility determinations.[56] In addition, OCE is responsible for ensuring that the tobacco products in provisional SE submissions found to be not substantially equivalent are no longer sold or distributed in the United States as of the date on the FDA-issued not substantially equivalent order.[57]

Table 5. State and Territorial Retail Inspection Contracts Awarded, Inspections Conducted, and Advisory and Enforcement Actions Taken by FDA as of March 31, 2014

Fiscal year	Cumulative number of states and territories awarded contracts[a]	Number of inspections	Warning letters issued	Civil monetary penalties assessed
2010	15	0	0	0
2011	40	24,404	1,022	1
2012	44	87,462	4,107	383
2013	45	109,906	5,992	535
2014[b]	45	57,474	3,107	428
Total	**45**	**279,246**	**14,228**	**1,347**

Source: GAO analysis of FDA data. | GAO-14-561

[a] This count includes the number of states and territories with a contract in each fiscal year.

[b] Data for fiscal year 2014 includes activities for the first two quarters (as of March 31, 2014).

Promotion, Advertising, and Labeling Surveillance

FDA also conducts surveillance activities for the promotion, advertising, and labeling of tobacco products. CTP's OCE conducts routine monitoring and surveillance of websites and social media, publications, and tobacco industry promotion and sponsorship of events that sell, distribute, promote, or advertise regulated tobacco products; and reviews and evaluates regulatory submissions of tobacco product labeling, advertising, and consumer information materials.[58] Additionally, CTP's OCE is responsible for ensuring that warning statements on smokeless tobacco product labeling and advertising are in compliance with requirements in the Tobacco Control Act, such as the packaging and advertising bearing the warning statement.[59] From fiscal year 2010 through March 31, 2014, OCE officials reported monitoring over 3,000 websites and over 68,000 issues of publications, resulting in 155 warning letters to manufacturers, distributors, and online retailers for violations. For example, warning letters were issued to (1) a website for selling clove cigarettes, a regulated tobacco product containing a characterizing flavor which is prohibited under the Tobacco Control Act; (2) a tobacco manufacturer for promoting the sale of cigarette tobacco (a regulated tobacco product) labeled as pipe tobacco (an unregulated tobacco product) on its website; and (3) a manufacturer for offering its tobacco products online as "light" and "mild" without an FDA order to market a modified risk tobacco product.

Outreach and Small Business Assistance

In addition to the three key compliance and enforcement activities mentioned above, CTP also conducts outreach and small business assistance activities to help ensure compliance with the Tobacco Control Act and regulations. OCE and its Office of Small Business Assistance are responsible for outreach and small business assistance. According to FDA officials, these activities include responding to inquiries from small manufacturers and retailers and providing information on relevant tobacco guidance and regulations, primarily through webinars that addressed certain topics, such as common issues identified during FDA's scientific evaluation of substantial equivalence reports and regulations regarding distribution of free samples of smokeless tobacco.

FDA ENCOUNTERED CHALLENGES AS IT ESTABLISHED CTP, INCLUDING SETTING REVIEW TIME FRAMES

FDA faced challenges related to starting up a new center, which affected CTP's efforts to educate the public, build the regulatory science base, and enforce the new law and regulations. While FDA officials indicated that the agency has taken steps to address some of the challenges it faced—such as those related to contracting and staffing—challenges related to building the scientific basis for regulating a previously unregulated product and setting review time frames remain. Despite these challenges, neither FDA officials nor public health and tobacco industry stakeholders identified any limitations in FDA's authority to carry out its responsibilities under the Tobacco Control Act.

According to CTP officials, one challenge FDA encountered, but which they believe the agency has addressed, was a lack of an acquisitions infrastructure that would allow it to quickly award contracts for public education activities. According to these officials, FDA had to develop a contracting mechanism of a sufficient size and scope to allow FDA to solicit and award large public education campaign contracts, which had never been done by the agency before. This process also included determining the type of contracts to award. The officials said that it took about 2 years before two pools of contractors were established, from which FDA could draw for future public education campaigns, delaying public education campaigns that were originally slated to launch in fiscal year 2012. CTP officials reported it was important to build an FDA contracting infrastructure for these campaigns, because public education activities are FDA's continuing responsibility. CTP officials stated that to decrease the toll of tobacco use on public health, public education activities must be managed by FDA, with a sustained fiscal and personnel commitment. While doing so delayed efforts to launch its public education campaigns, CTP officials told us they do not expect similar delays in the future.

Additionally, according to CTP officials, CTP's OCE faced initial challenges in getting up and running—in particular in setting up the retailer inspection program, including the contracts for the program. According to CTP officials, in a very short period of time and with limited staff in place, CTP's OCE had to draft an initial request for proposals to award contracts to states and help them navigate through the contracting process, commission state and territorial officials to conduct retail compliance inspections, develop and implement training programs for inspectors, coordinators, and retailers, and develop a new information technology system to collect and report retailer compliance inspection data. However, these officials reported that since the early stages of the tobacco program, the center has built a strong FDA tobacco compliance and enforcement infrastructure, and noted that if additional tobacco products are deemed to fall under the authority of CTP, they should be able to expand and cover them relatively easily.

CTP officials also reported FDA has taken steps to address challenges stemming from staffing and information technology that slowed the development and implementation of the product review processes needed for regulating tobacco products. In 2013, we reported that a shortage of experienced staff and challenges finding qualified staff contributed to long review times for new tobacco product submissions.[60] CTP officials reported that the training of OS staff for product reviews will always be challenging because much of the training must be on-the-job, but they do not expect that this challenge will be an impediment to conducting new tobacco product and MRTP reviews. To help prepare OS staff for conducting reviews, CTP has drafted reviewer's guides, which identify specific procedures staff should implement in each step of review. CTP officials also reported that OS—the office responsible for new tobacco product reviews—increased the number of positions over time from 18 in fiscal year 2010 to 205 in fiscal year 2014, and that they do not expect that finding qualified staff will be a challenge for OS moving forward (see Figure 7).[61] (For information on CTP positions by office, see app. III.)

Tobacco industry stakeholders expressed concerns, however, about whether CTP will have a sufficient number of staff to review the backlog of the more than 4,000 new tobacco product submissions received as of March 31, 2014, and also review new submissions that may be made in the future, particularly if new types of tobacco products—such as cigars or e-cigarettes—are deemed to be subject to FDA's regulatory authority as the agency has proposed. In addition, CTP officials reported that a slow information technology system impacted the rate at which staff could enter data during reviews of SE submissions, which slowed down review times for such submissions. CTP officials told us that in January 2014, CTP deployed a new information technology system (known as the Office of Science Review Information System) to support the tracking, management, and review of submissions. They told us they expect this new system to provide for more efficient oversight of reviews, and they expect to use the system if new types of tobacco products are deemed to be subject to FDA's regulatory authority.

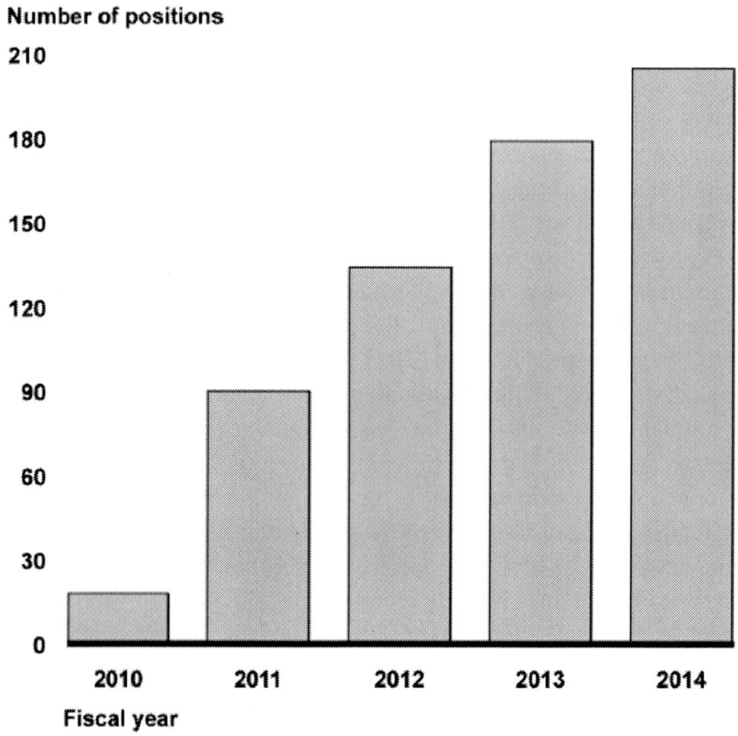

Source: GAO summary of FDA information. | GAO-14-561.
Notes: Information for fiscal year 2014 is as of March 31, 2014.
According to CTP, there were no OS staff in fiscal year 2009. Positions include students and consultants, including special government employees, at the end of each fiscal year.

Figure 7. Center for Tobacco Products (CTP) Office of Science (OS) Positions as of March 31, 2014.

FDA will continue to face challenges as it conducts regulatory science activities for what FDA considers to be a complex product that had not been subject to previous regulation. The following examples illustrate the continuing challenges related to implementing a tobacco product review process, building the scientific research base, and building the scientific basis to support regulations and guidance:

- *Novel issues in submissions*. CTP officials told us that product reviews continue to have novel issues that OS officials need to carefully consider in light of establishing precedent for future reviews. They said that this will continue to be a challenge as OS staff conduct additional reviews and tobacco manufacturers make changes to their products.

- *Incomplete submissions*. CTP officials also reported that SE submissions for new tobacco products have been challenging to review because they have not been complete. Industry stakeholders reported that determining and providing what CTP would consider sufficient information in SE submissions has been challenging because FDA's guidance has been lacking. For example, as we previously reported, industry stakeholders told us that the SE guidance document issued by FDA in January 2011 did not direct manufacturers to include some information, such as environmental assessments, that CTP later requested from manufacturers in its September 2011 draft guidance or through direct communication with manufacturers. CTP officials noted that the agency has made efforts to publish additional guidance and conduct webinars to address the issue and that they plan to develop a standardized form for manufacturers to use when submitting information for review. According to CTP officials, as of April 25, 2014, CTP was developing a proposed regulation on the content and format of SE submissions, but the center could not identify an estimated time frame for implementing such a regulation. CTP officials noted that they have begun seeing some overall improvement in submissions, but they expect that incomplete submissions will continue to be a challenge moving forward.
- *Regulating menthol in cigarettes*. According to FDA officials, the issue of menthol in cigarettes is complex and there is a broad range of scientific evidence on the issue. As a result, FDA has not acted on findings from the Tobacco Products Scientific Advisory Committee's 2011 report that the removal of menthol cigarettes from the market would benefit public health, nor has it acted on the findings from its own additional, independent evaluation on menthol, which took an additional 2 years before the agency issued an advanced notice of proposed rulemaking. According to public health stakeholders, FDA could have taken action on menthol in cigarettes based on the 2011 report from the Tobacco Products Scientific Advisory Committee. In July 2013, about 4 years after the passage of the Tobacco Control Act and about 2 years after the release of the advisory committee report, FDA issued an Advanced Notice of Proposed Rule Making to obtain

comments on its evaluation and on potential regulatory action. According to CTP officials, as of March 25, 2014, FDA was in the process of reviewing what it considers to be an unusually large number of comments—174,000—received in response to the notice.

- *Reporting HPHC data to the public.* FDA officials stated that the agency needs to evaluate the quality of HPHC data and conduct more research before it can meet the Tobacco Control Act requirement to provide the public with understandable and not misleading information regarding HPHCs in tobacco products. While CTP has established a list of HPHCs, FDA has not released HPHC information to the public by the April 1, 2013, deadline required in the act because, according to CTP officials, the center has needed to evaluate the quality of HPHC data collected from manufacturers and the center does not yet have sufficient evidence that the HPHC data can be presented to consumers in an understandable way that is not misleading. Industry stakeholders stated that because CTP has not provided standards or regulations for how HPHC testing should be conducted, the HPHC data that manufacturers have spent time and money producing for FDA may not be useful because of the variation in testing methods used by manufacturers. According to CTP officials, CTP is developing a proposed regulation related to manufacturers' testing and reporting of HPHC data. The Tobacco Products Scientific Advisory Committee and FDA's Risk Communication Advisory Committee made recommendations on further research and strategies to communicate HPHC information in public education campaigns to help consumers make informed decisions about tobacco products, and according to CTP officials, FDA does not plan to release its list of HPHCs that will be understandable and not misleading to the public as required by the Tobacco Control Act until additional research is completed.[62] As of June 4, 2014, CTP officials had not publicly disclosed an updated timeline for developing a proposed regulation related to the testing and reporting of HPHCs, but indicated it plans to do so.
- *Regulating other tobacco products.* According to CTP officials, there is much that needs to be learned about the types of tobacco products that FDA does not currently regulate, and FDA will not be able to obtain some information about these types of products until they are subject to FDA's authority and FDA can require that manufacturers provide the information. However, the agency conducted research and

developed information regarding these products in order to propose deeming additional types of tobacco products to be subject to its regulatory authority.[63] In April 2014—about 3 years after FDA announced its intention to deem additional types of tobacco products to be subject to its regulatory authority—FDA issued a notice of proposed rulemaking that would subject other types of tobacco products, such as e-cigarettes, to federal regulations, including minimum age requirements.[64] In the view of public health stakeholders, FDA has moved too slowly to deem additional tobacco products to be subject to its authority, allowing new types of tobacco products that stakeholders believe negatively impact public health to enter the U.S. market. However, CTP officials said that agencies must comply with certain requirements in developing regulations and that FDA was required to meet these requirements before issuing a proposed rule. In addition, the officials explained that FDA spent a significant amount of time ensuring that support for its proposed regulation to deem additional tobacco products subject to the agency's authority was strong and complete, which included spending time ensuring a strong scientific underpinning for regulation.

Finally, relating to the product review processes, we have previously recommended that FDA establish and monitor performance measures for its review of new tobacco product submissions.[65] Specifically, in September 2013, we recommended that FDA establish performance measures that include time frames for making decisions on new tobacco product submissions, and monitor performance relative to the established time frames, to allow CTP to evaluate its efficiency and effectiveness and help it make appropriate adjustments.[66] HHS agreed with our recommendation, and on April 18, 2014, announced new performance measures for regular SE submissions, Exemption from SE submissions, and MRTP submissions received in fiscal years 2015 through 2018, meaning that FDA will start monitoring the time it takes to review and take action on these submissions.[67] FDA has not, however, specified when it will establish time frames for provisional SE submissions—the type of SE submission that comprises the bulk of submissions received by FDA and that represent new tobacco products that may continue to be marketed unless and until CTP finds that they are not substantially equivalent. According to FDA, as the agency gains more experience with reviewing provisional SE submissions, it intends to identify and implement performance standards for these submissions as well.[68] The continued lack of time frames for reviews of provisional SE submissions will limit CTP's ability to evaluate policies, procedures, and staffing resources in relation to CTP's review process for provisional SE submissions and, in turn, limit CTP's ability to reasonably assure efficient operations and effective results.

CONCLUDING OBSERVATIONS

In the 5 years since the Tobacco Control Act was enacted, FDA has set up a new center and undertaken numerous activities to regulate a previously unregulated product using a public health standard, and the agency remains in the process of conducting research and setting up its regulatory structure. FDA has taken some steps to address our previous recommendation to institute performance measures for its review of new tobacco products by establishing time frames for regular SE and Exemption from SE submissions, as well as for MRTP submissions, and by planning to monitor its progress towards meeting those time frames. However, we remain concerned that the agency has not yet established any performance measures for the more than 3,000 provisional SE submissions, representing tobacco products that can stay on the market unless and until FDA finds them not substantially equivalent. It is important that the agency move forward on reviewing these submissions—particularly, those that FDA has identified as having the greatest potential to have a public health impact—to ensure that only products that meet the act's requirements are permitted to be on the market. The agency has indicated that it intends to identify and implement performance measures for these provisional SE submissions as it gains more experience reviewing them. We continue to believe that until FDA establishes performance measures including time frames for completing reviews of the large backlog of provisional SE submissions, the agency's ability to operate efficiently, achieve effective results, and plan appropriately will be hampered. This will be particularly pressing as FDA moves forward with plans to deem additional types of tobacco products to be subject to its regulatory authority, which has the potential to generate a substantial number of new submissions requiring review. Similarly, it will be important for the agency to establish time frames for submissions for any newly deemed products, as FDA has indicated that the just-released time frames will not apply to submissions for newly-deemed products.

AGENCY COMMENTS

We provided a draft of this report to HHS for comment. HHS agreed with the need for performance measures related to its new tobacco product review process. In its comments, the department noted several reasons why it has been difficult for FDA to set performance measures for provisional SE submissions. According to HHS, FDA received a large number of provisional SE submissions in a short period of time, which required the agency to prioritize the review process based on the complexity of the public health concerns likely to be raised by the products under review. As a result, HHS noted that the initial reviews are more complicated, with unpredictable time frames. Additionally, because provisional SE submissions were received early in CTP's SE review process, HHS commented that many submissions have deficiencies that require corrections from manufacturers and further slows the review and approval process. However, HHS noted that the knowledge gained during the review of provisional SE submissions will inform the process in the future and allow FDA to eventually set performance goals for these submissions.

While we acknowledge there are complexities to the provisional SE review process, we believe that it is critical that FDA set performance measures for managing the review process of provisional SE submissions, including establishing time frames for review and monitoring progress toward meeting those time frames. Since these products can remain on the market unless and until FDA determines they are not substantially equivalent, it is important for FDA to effectively manage the review of these products to fulfill its responsibility to protect the public health.

HHS also provided technical comments that were incorporated, as appropriate.

Marcia Crosse
Director, Health Care

APPENDIX I: SUMMARY OF CENTER FOR TOBACCO PRODUCTS OFFICES AND KEY ACTIVITIES

This appendix provides a summary of the offices that comprise the Food and Drug Administration's (FDA) Center for Tobacco Products (CTP), their key activities, spending on each key activity, and examples of activities through March 31, 2014 (see table 6).

Table 6. Summary of Center for Tobacco Products (CTP) Offices, Spending, and Key Activities as of March 31, 2014

CTP office and key activities	Spending in fiscal years 2010-2014[a] (in millions)	Examples of activities
Office of the Center Director		
Leadership and Management	$16	• Oversee all tobacco program operations
Office of Compliance and Enforcement		
Tobacco Retailer Inspections	$123	• Contract with states and territories for tobacco retailer inspections • Commission and train inspection program participants • Conduct advisory and enforcement actions in response to Tobacco Control Act violations
Manufacturer and Import Inspections and Enforcement[b]	$36	• Conduct inspections of domestic tobacco manufacturers • Implement and enforce import compliance program for tobacco products

CTP office and key activities	Spending in fiscal years 2010-2014[a] (in millions)	Examples of activities
		• Consult with CTP's Office of Science on status of predicate product cited in substantial equivalence submissions
Promotion, Advertising, and Labeling Surveillance	$19	• Surveillance of tobacco product websites and social media • Surveillance of tobacco product advertisements in magazines and other publications • Review of tobacco labeling and advertising submissions
Outreach and Small Business Assistance	$3	• Respond to questions from small businesses and retailers • Provide educational webinars on relevant tobacco regulation and guidance topics for small businesses and retailers
Office of Health Communication and Education		
Public Education Campaigns	$450	• Establish contracting mechanism for multi-year tobacco education campaigns • Launch initial youth campaigns • Develop and implement retailer education campaign on new tobacco laws and regulations • Fund research to inform and improve campaigns
Communicating CTP Activities	$58	• Educate and inform key audiences about CTP's creation, FDA's authorities over tobacco, and its work related to tobacco regulation

Table 6. (Continued)

CTP office and key activities	Spending in fiscal years 2010-2014[a] (in millions)	Examples of activities
Office of Management		
Administrative Services	$47	• Manage administrative programs such as travel, CTP Document Control Center, acquisitions, training, safety and security, organization changes, and emergency planning • Establish office spend plans to budget CTP funds according to strategic center priorities • Establish administrative infrastructure for partnership with the National Institutes of Health
Office of Policy[c]		
Policy, Research Analysis, and Liaison Activity	$28	• Host listening sessions with members of industry • Represent CTP at external public health stakeholder and industry meetings • Conduct outreach calls to public health stakeholders and members of industry
Office of Regulations		
Issue Guidance	$4	• Issue revised draft guidance on compliance with reissued 1996 rule • Issue draft guidance on tobacco retailer training programs and civil monetary penalties • Issue final guidance regarding use of light, mild, low, and similar descriptors; substantial equivalence

CTP office and key activities	Spending in fiscal years 2010-2014[a] (in millions)	Examples of activities
		submissions; harmful and potentially harmful constituents (HPHC) in tobacco products and tobacco smoke
Issue Regulations	$14	• Reissue 1996 rule establishing restrictions on the sale and promotion of cigarettes and smokeless tobacco products • Issue final rule requiring graphic warnings on cigarette packages and in cigarette advertising • Clear proposed rule establishing requirements for submission of data needed to calculate user fees for manufacturers and importers
Office of Science		
Building a Scientific Research Base	$449	• Coordinate with federal agencies to develop a tobacco research plan/strategy for providing the scientific research base needed to inform FDA's regulatory decisions • Design and conduct an experimental study to test the relative effectiveness of graphic warnings • Meet with manufacturers on the science of smoked, smokeless, and dissolvable tobacco products and e-cigarettes, and conduct manufacturer site visits to learn more about the manufacturing, marketing, and distribution of tobacco products

Table 6. (Continued)

CTP office and key activities	Spending in fiscal years 2010-2014[a] (in millions)	Examples of activities
		• Conduct focus groups with adults and youth on their understanding and interpretation of HPHCs and conduct an experimental study to test the effects of HPHC lists on consumer understanding and perceptions of tobacco products • Fund research at federal agencies and other private entities to better understand tobacco products, health effects, use patterns, and risk perceptions
Developing and Implementing a Tobacco Product Review Process	$25	• Develop and implement process for review and evaluation for Substantial Equivalence (SE) submissions • Review SE submissions, modified risk tobacco product applications, investigational use, postmarket, and premarket tobacco product applications • Hold webinars to update industry on SE submissions • Design and implement a system to receive, process, and assess tobacco product adverse event and product problem reports • Host two Tobacco Products Scientific Advisory Committee meetings related to modified risk tobacco products

CTP office and key activities	Spending in fiscal years 2010-2014[a](in millions)	Examples of activities
Regulation and Guidance Support	$5	• Host Tobacco Products Scientific Advisory Committee meetings to address statutory requirements • Publish (draft) guidance, including guidance on applications for premarket review of new tobacco products and industry reporting of HPHCs • Hold public workshops; e.g., tobacco product analysis • Issue advanced notices of proposed rulemaking

Source: GAO summary of FDA information. | GAO-14-561

Notes: Spending for compliance and enforcement activities includes tobacco-related spending of FDA's Office of Regulatory Affairs.

[a] Information for fiscal year 2014 includes activities for the first two quarters (as of March 31, 2014).

[b] Includes the tobacco-related spending of FDA's Office of Regulatory Affairs.

[c] According to CTP officials, as a result of an organizational review, entities within the Office of Policy were reassigned as of April 1, 2014, to the Office of the Center Director, the Office of Management, and the Office of Science.

Appendix II: Examples of Tobacco-Related Research Projects Supported by Food and Drug Administration Spending

This appendix provides examples of research projects supported by the Food and Drug Administration (FDA) spending of tobacco user fees in fiscal years 2010 through March 31, 2014. Although FDA spending supported these research projects, in addition to FDA, other federal agencies, such as the National Institutes of Health (NIH) or the Centers for Disease Control and Prevention (CDC), as well as non-federal entities, such as research institutes, conducted or had oversight over these research projects (see table 7).

Table 7. Examples of Tobacco-Related Research Projects Supported by FDA Spending and the Entity Conducting or Overseeing the Project as of March 31, 2014

Fiscal year	Research project examples (*entity conducting or overseeing project*)
2010	• Marketing of New Tobacco Product Use Among Adults (*NIH*) • National Youth Tobacco Survey (*CDC*) • Brand Comparison of 50 Tobacco Products (*CDC*) • Experimental Study for Cigarette Graphic Health Warnings (*Non-federal entity*) • Focus Groups on Tobacco Products and HPHCs[a](*Non-federal entity*)
2011	• Uptake of Carcinogens by Menthol Cigarette Smokers (*NIH*) • Evaluating the Toxicity and Inflammation in Human Tissue Produced by Tobacco Products (*FDA*) • National Youth Tobacco Survey (*CDC*) • Brand Comparison of 50 Tobacco Products (*CDC*) • Influences on Tobacco Use Decisions (*Non-federal entity*) • Experimental Study of Emerging Tobacco Products (*Non-federal entity*) • Experimental Study on Presentation of HPHCs[a](*Non-federal entity*)
2012	• Rapid Response Human Testing of Smokeless Tobacco Products (*NIH*) • Survey of Microbes in Snuff Smokeless Tobacco Products (*FDA*) • National Youth Tobacco Survey (*CDC*)

Fiscal year	Research project examples (*entity conducting or overseeing project*)
	• Brand Comparison of 50 Tobacco Products (*CDC*) • Experimental Study on Little Cigar Topography (*Non-federal entity*) • Data on Poison Events Associated with Tobacco Products (*Non-federal entity*) • Epidemiological Studies of Tobacco Use and Cardiovascular Outcomes (*Non-federal entity*) • Focus Groups on Hookah, E-Cigarettes (*Non-federal entity*)
2013	• The Impact of Tobacco Exposure on the Lungs (*NIH*) • Market Research to Predict Emerging Tobacco Product Use in Diverse Young Adults (*NIH*) • Influence of Advertising and Product Type on E-Cigarette Demand among Smokers (*NIH*) • Biomarkers for Bladder Cancer Associated with Tobacco Smoke (*FDA*) • National Youth Tobacco Survey (*CDC*) • Brand Comparison of 50 Tobacco Products (*CDC*) • Population Assessment of Tobacco and Health Study (*Non-federal entity*) • Assessment of Tobacco Pharmacology and Behavior in Humans (*Non-federal entity*)
2014[b]	• Genetic Biomarkers of Nicotine Addictions (*NIH*) • Effects of Hookah Tobacco Smoke in the Human Respiratory System (*NIH*) • Expansion of National Youth Tobacco Survey (*CDC*) • Harmful and Potentially Harmful Constituent Method Development and Baseline Analysis (*CDC*) • Biomarkers for Tobacco Smoke Associated with Bladder Cancer (*FDA*) • Nicotine Self-Administration in Rodents (*FDA*) • Pharmacokinetics and Topography of E-Cigarettes (*Non-federal entity*)

Source: GAO analysis of FDA information. | GAO-14-561

Note: Non-federal entities include, for example, the Research Triangle Institute International, American Association of Poison Control Centers, American College of Cardiology, and Battelle Memorial Institute.

[a] HPHC stands for harmful and potentially harmful constituent.

[b] Information for fiscal year 2014 includes examples for the first two quarters (as of March 31, 2014).

APPENDIX III: POSITIONS AT THE CENTER FOR TOBACCO PRODUCTS (CTP) AT THE END OF EACH FISCAL YEAR AS OF MARCH 31, 2014

Office	Fiscal year					
	2009	2010	2011	2012	2013	2014[a]
Office of Health Communication and Education	0	14	33	37	47	49
Office of Science	0	18	90	134	179	205
Office of Compliance and Enforcement	0	37	79	101	117	151
Other CTP Offices[b]	1	74	128	155	159	153
Total	**1**	**143**	**330**	**427**	**502**	**558**

Source: GAO analysis of FDA data. | GAO-14-561

Notes: Position numbers include students and consultants, including special government employees.

[a] Data for fiscal year 2014 includes activities for the first two quarters (as of March 31, 2014).

[b] Other CTP offices include the Office of the Center Director, the Office of Management, the Office of Policy, and the Office of Regulations. According to CTP officials, as a result of an organizational review, entities within the Office of Policy were reassigned as of April 1, 2014, to the Office of the Center Director, the Office of Management, and the Office of Science.

End Notes

[1] Department of Health and Human Services, *The Health Consequences of Smoking— 50 Years of Progress: A Report of the Surgeon General* (Atlanta, Ga.: Jan. 17, 2014).

[2] Pub. L. No. 111-31, div. A, 123 Stat. 1776 (2009). Tobacco products that FDA currently regulates include cigarettes, cigarette tobacco, roll-your-own tobacco, and smokeless tobacco products. The Tobacco Control Act enables FDA to assert jurisdiction over other tobacco products through rulemaking. Under the public health standard, FDA regulates tobacco products for the protection of the public health, taking into account the risks and benefits of tobacco products on the population as a whole, including users and non-users.

[3] § 101(b), 123 Stat. at 1787 (codified at 21 U.S.C. § 387a(e)).

[4] § 101(b), 123 Stat. at 1826 (codified at 21 U.S.C. § 387s).

[5] § 106 (b), 123 Stat. at 1842 (codified at 21 U.S.C. § 387u(b)).

[6] For the purposes of this report, spending means obligations, including those for which expenditures have been made. The term obligation refers to a definite commitment by a federal agency that creates a legal liability to make payments immediately or in the future. According to FDA, CTP spent $4.9 million in the fourth quarter of fiscal year 2009 for startup activities. The center, which was established in August 2009, did not report fiscal year 2009 spending by office or activity.

[7] § 101(b), 123 Stat. at 1786 (codified at 21 U.S.C. § 387a). Tobacco products that FDA currently regulates include cigarettes, cigarette tobacco, roll-your-own tobacco, and smokeless tobacco products. The Tobacco Control Act enables FDA to deem other products that are made or derived from tobacco and intended for human consumption—for example, cigars, pipe tobacco, hookah, and e-cigarettes—subject to its authority by rulemaking.

[8] § 101(b), 123 Stat. at 1796, 1803 (codified at 21 U.S.C. §§ 387f(d)(3), 387g(d)(3)). Section 104 of the act directs FDA to convene an expert panel to conduct a study on the public health implications of raising the minimum age to purchase tobacco and to submit a report to Congress by April 2015. According to CTP officials, FDA has contracted with the Institute of Medicine to empanel a committee of experts and develop a report for CTP by January 2015. The Institute of Medicine report will be used as a basis for FDA's report to Congress.

[9] § 102(a), 123 Stat. at 1830 (codified at 21 U.S.C. § 387a-1(a)). FDA reissued this final rule in March 2010. 75 Fed. Reg. 13,225 (Mar. 19, 2010).

[10] §§ 101(b), 201(a), 123 Stat. at 1799, 1845 (codified at 21 U.S.C. § 387g(a)(1)(A) and 15 U.S.C. § 1533(d)). While the Tobacco Control Act explicitly exempted menthol from the flavor ban, it required additional research on the public health impact of menthol in cigarettes and gave FDA the authority to ban menthol if it finds such a ban is appropriate for the protection of the public health. § 101(b), 123 Stat. at 1804 (codified at 21 U.S.C. § 387g(e)). In June 2011, FDA issued a final rule specifying nine color graphic images to accompany new textual warnings for cigarette packages and advertisements. 76 Fed. Reg. 36,628 (June 22, 2011). In February 2012, however, a federal appeals court found that FDA failed to provide substantial evidence that the rule's specific requirements would reduce the number of Americans who smoke and, therefore, that the rule unconstitutionally restricted cigarette manufacturers' First Amendment rights. The court vacated the rule and remanded it to FDA. *R.J. Reynolds Tobacco Co. v. F.D.A.*, 696 F.3d 1205 (D.C. Cir. 2012). FDA did not appeal the court's decision. As of April 25, 2014, FDA has not issued a revised rule, but indicated plans to conduct research in an effort to do so.

[11] A predicate tobacco product is a product commercially marketed in the United States on February 15, 2007, or previously found by FDA to be substantially equivalent, provided the product has not been removed from the market at FDA's initiative or has not been determined by a judicial order to be misbranded or adulterated.

[12] Manufacturers can make a submission under the Exemption from SE pathway if the product is modified by adding, deleting, or changing the quantity of an additive and (1) the new product is a minor modification of another tobacco product marketed by the same manufacturer; (2) an SE submission is not necessary to ensure that permitting the tobacco product to be marketed would be appropriate for the protection of the public health; and (3) an Exemption from SE is otherwise appropriate.

[13] The PMTA submission must include, among other things, full reports of investigations of health risks, and must meet the public health standard described under the Tobacco Control Act. To determine whether marketing of a new tobacco product would be appropriate for the protection of the public health, CTP applies standards that take into account the risks and benefits to the population as a whole, including the likelihood that existing users of tobacco products will stop using such products and the likelihood that those who do not use tobacco products will start using such products.

[14] § 101(b), 123 Stat. at 1812 (codified at 21 U.S.C. § 387k). MRTPs can only be legally marketed after FDA issues an order permitting their marketing.

[15] §§ 6, 101(b), 123 Stat. at 1783, 1791 (codified at 21 U.S.C. §§ 387d(a)(3), (e)). Manufacturers are required to report HPHC data at least 90 days prior to introducing a tobacco product that was not on the market on June 22, 2009.

[16] §§ 6, 101(b), 123 Stat. at 1783, 1790-91 (codified at 21 U.S.C. § 387d(d)).

[17] § 101(b), 123 Stat. at 1804 (codified at 21 U.S.C. § 387g(e)). The Tobacco Control Act established the Tobacco Products Scientific Advisory Committee, a 12-member advisory committee, to review and evaluate safety, dependence, and health issues relating to tobacco

products and provide appropriate advice, information, and recommendations to FDA for tobacco-related regulations. Tobacco Control Act, § 101(b), 123 Stat. at 1824 (codified at 21 U.S.C. § 387q). The committee was established on March 23, 2010.

[18] § 101(b), 123 Stat. at 1826-28 (codified at 21 U.S.C. § 387s(b)-(c)). Tobacco products subject to FDA regulation include those products specified in the Tobacco Control Act—cigarettes, cigarette tobacco, roll-your-own tobacco, and smokeless tobacco—and any other tobacco products that FDA deems to be subject to its authority. User fees are a fee assessed to users for goods or services provided by the federal government. The Tobacco Control Act specified the total amount of user fees authorized to be collected for each fiscal year beginning with fiscal year 2009, and authorized user fees to remain available until expended (which means that FDA may carry over user fees to subsequent fiscal years if they are not obligated by the end of the fiscal year in which they were collected). Fees are collected and available for obligation only to the extent and in the amount provided in advance in appropriations acts. For fiscal year 2014, Congress appropriated $534 million in tobacco user fees for collection and obligation—the total amount authorized under the Tobacco Control Act.

[19] ORA assists with CTP's compliance activities by inspecting regulated products and manufacturers, conducting sample analyses of regulated products, and reviewing imported products offered for entry into the United States.

[20] In addition to the work carried out by CTP and ORA, tobacco user fees also support U.S. General Services Administration rent, other rent, and rent-related activities and other tobacco-related activities carried out by FDA, including headquarters and the Office of the Commissioner.

[21] Data include spending for CTP overhead (information technology infrastructure and centralized funding for, among other things, furniture, office equipment, and center-wide training); ORA; tobacco-related spending of FDA headquarters and the Office of the Commissioner; and General Services Administration rent, other rent, and rent-related activities.

[22] According to CTP officials, FDA is on track to meet its fiscal year 2014 spend plan; 80 percent of the planned acquisitions items will be awarded in the second half of the fiscal year, per FDA acquisition deadlines. Additionally, officials noted that the majority of the reimbursements for ORA, FDA headquarters, and the Office of the Commissioner will also take place in the second half of the fiscal year.

[23] See GAO, *New Tobacco Products: FDA Needs to Set Time Frames for Its Review Process*, GAO-13-723 (Washington, D.C.: Sept. 6, 2013).

[24] FDA officials noted there are multiple agencies that conduct activities related to tobacco issues, including public education activities. To avoid duplication, CTP participates in an HHS tobacco control working group that meets monthly. The working group includes representatives from the Office of the Surgeon General, Centers for Disease Control and Prevention, Health Resources and Services Administration, and the Office of the Assistant Secretary for Health, among others.

[25] Information on FDA's campaign can be found at "The Real Cost Campaign," accessed May 6, 2014, http://www.fda.gov/TheRealCost.

[26] We have previously reported on the importance of developing a systematic approach to designing program evaluations in order to enhance the credibility of the evaluation and ensure resources are being used effectively (see GAO, *Designing Evaluations: 2012 Revision*, GAO-12-208G (Washington, D.C.: Jan. 2012)). We have also reported on the difficulties associated with evaluating public communications campaigns (see, for example, GAO, *ONDCP Media Campaign: Contractor's National Evaluation Did Not Find that the Youth Anti-Drug Media Campaign Was Effective in Reducing Youth Drug Use*, GAO-06-818 (Washington, D.C.: Aug. 25, 2006)).

[27] Spending on building the scientific research base has primarily been through grants and contracts, while product review spending represents staffing within CTP.

[28] CTP officials reported plans to continue research to show that graphic warning labels will benefit public health; however, they did not have a time frame for completing the research or issuing a new graphic warning label regulation following a February 2012 federal appeals court decision that vacated the agency's original rule.

[29] The Population Assessment of Tobacco and Health study started to enroll participants in September 2013 and plans to enroll up to 59,000 people (both tobacco users and non-users) ages 12 and older.

[30] Department of Health and Human Services, Food and Drug Administration, "FDA and NIH Study: Population Assessment of Tobacco and Health," accessed April 24, 2014, http://www.fda.gov/TobaccoProducts/PublicHealthScienceResearch/ucm337005.htm.

[31] Department of Health and Human Services, Food and Drug Administration, "Tobacco Centers of Regulatory Science," accessed April 24, 2014, http://www.fda.gov/TobaccoProducts/PublicHealthScienceResearch/ucm369005.htm. The 14 Tobacco Centers of Regulatory Science include scientists with a broad range of expertise, including epidemiology, economics, toxicology, addictions, and marketing, located primarily within universities.

[32] On April 25, 2014, FDA issued a proposed rule that, if finalized, would deem all products that meet the statutory definition of a tobacco product—including currently unregulated marketed products, such as e-cigarettes, cigars, pipe tobacco, nicotine gels, waterpipe (or hookah) tobacco, and dissolvables—to be subject to FDA's regulation under the Tobacco Control Act. 79 Fed. Reg. 23,142 (Apr. 25, 2014).

[33] For additional information on FDA's new tobacco product review process, see GAO-13-723.

[34] Regular SE submissions are for new tobacco products not yet commercially marketed. Regular SE submissions were received by FDA after March 22, 2011. The tobacco products represented in these submissions may not be marketed until CTP issues an order that they are substantially equivalent.

[35] As of March 31, 2014, CTP had refused to accept 36 of the 61 Exemption from SE submissions received by FDA because the submissions did not meet statutory requirements. CTP had refused to file the 4 PMTA submissions FDA had received as of that date. According to CTP officials and industry representatives, one reason for the lack of submissions under the PMTA pathway may be the challenge in demonstrating that a manufacturer has met the public health standard (appropriate for the protection of the public health) for the PMTA pathway. See http://www.fda.gov/TobaccoProducts/Labeling/MarketingandAdvertising/ucm339928.htm, accessed April 10, 2014, for information on FDA's tobacco product marketing orders.

[36] Provisional SE submissions are for new tobacco products commercially marketed after February 15, 2007, but before March 22, 2011. Provisional SE submissions were received by FDA by March 22, 2011. The tobacco products represented in these submissions may be commercially marketed unless and until FDA issues an order that they are not substantially equivalent.

[37] As of March 31, 2014, CTP received 70 submissions regarding investigational use of tobacco products; 62 have completed review and 8 were pending review. In addition, CTP reviewed 62 correspondences regarding investigational use of a tobacco product. Under the Tobacco Control Act, FDA may exempt tobacco products intended for investigational use from these requirements under conditions as FDA may prescribe by regulation. § 101(b), 123 Stat. at 1812 (codified at 21 U.S.C. § 387j(g)). As of March 31, 2014, however, FDA had not issued such regulations, and FDA was exercising enforcement discretion for the premarket review requirements when investigators can ensure that studies on the tobacco product are well-controlled, data derived from such studies are reliable, and study subjects are adequately protected. In addition, the investigational tobacco product should not be promoted, advertised, distributed, commercially marketed, and/or sold to consumers.

[38] In addition, CTP officials reported that there were two other reasons for prioritizing regular SE submissions over provisional SE submissions: FDA received a large number of provisional SE submissions on March 21, 2011 (the day before the statutory deadline for submitting

provisional SE submissions), making it impractical to prioritize reviews by the date the submission was received; and CTP required time to assess which approach to reviewing provisional submissions would be the most effective at addressing the public health burden of tobacco use.

[39] The FDA/NIH Safety Reporting Portal is used by consumers, healthcare professionals, and other individuals to report safety concerns about products such as medical products, foods, cosmetics, and veterinary products. HHS, the Department of Defense, and the Department of Veterans Affairs created the portal to improve coordination among federal agencies for adverse event and product problem reporting.

[40] Department of Health and Human Services, Food and Drug Administration, Tobacco Products Scientific Advisory Committee, *Menthol Cigarettes and Public Health: Review of the Scientific Evidence and Recommendations* (Silver Spring, Md.: Mar. 23, 2011).

[41] Department of Health and Human Services, Food and Drug Administration, *Preliminary Scientific Evaluation of the Possible Public Health Effects of Menthol Versus Nonmenthol Cigarettes*, accessed April 14, 2014, http://www.fda.gov/downloads/ScienceResearch/SpecialTopics/PeerReviewofScientificInformationandAssessments/UCM361598.pdf.

[42] 78 Fed. Reg. 44,484 (July 24, 2013).

[43] 77 Fed. Reg. 20,034 (Apr. 3, 2012).

[44] Department of Health and Human Services, Food and Drug Administration, Center for Tobacco Products, *Draft Guidance for Industry: Reporting Harmful and Potentially Harmful Constituents in Tobacco Products and Tobacco Smoke Under Section 904(a)(3) of the Federal Food, Drug, and Cosmetic Act* (Silver Spring, Md.: March 2012). In its draft guidance, FDA noted that given the short time frame between issuance of the draft guidance and the required HPHC reporting date, FDA did not intend to enforce the statutory requirement for manufacturers to provide data on all HPHCs; rather, FDA established an abbreviated list of HPHCs for manufacturers to use for initially reporting HPHC data. According to the draft guidance, FDA will implement and enforce the statutory requirement to report all HPHCs on FDA's list "as appropriate." FDA issued a public notice describing the criteria the agency had tentatively concluded it would use to assist the agency in identifying HPHCs and listing 96 HPHCs the agency had identified using those criteria, in August 2011. 76 Fed. Reg. 50,226 (Aug. 12, 2011).

[45] § 101(b), 123 Stat. at 1791 (codified at 21 U.S.C. § 387d(d)).

[46] FDA announced this planned publication date in the *Fall 2013 Regulatory Plan and the Unified Agenda of Federal Regulatory and Deregulatory Actions*, accessed June 9, 2014, http://www.reginfo.gov/public/do/eAgendaViewRule?pubId=201310&RIN=0910-AG59. According to HHS, as of June 4, 2014, the agency plans to update the estimated publication date in the next edition of the Unified Agenda.

[47] Department of Health and Human Services, Food and Drug Administration, *Section 905(j) Reports: Demonstrating Substantial Equivalence for Tobacco Products* (Silver Spring, Md.: Jan. 5, 2011).

[48] Department of Health and Human Services, Food and Drug Administration, Center for Tobacco Products, *Draft Guidance for Industry and FDA Staff Demonstrating The Substantial Equivalence of a New Tobacco Product: Responses to Frequently Asked Questions* (Silver Spring, Md.: Sept. 22, 2011).

[49] The Tobacco Control Act directs FDA, to the extent feasible, to contract with states and territories to carry out inspections of tobacco retailers in connection with enforcement of the act. § 103(g), 123 Stat. at 1837 (codified at 21 U.S.C. § 372(a)(1)(B)).

[50] FDA may impose a no-tobacco-sale order prohibiting the sale of tobacco products at retail outlets that have committed repeated violations of the law. § 103(c), 123 Stat. at 1835 (codified at 21 U.S.C. § 333(f)(8)). According to FDA officials, other enforcement actions can include seizures, injunctions, and criminal prosecution.

[51] FDA plans to collaborate with tribal communities to contract with the agency to enforce regulations on tribal lands. According to FDA, the agency has contracted with an American

Indian-owned company to further its efforts to collaborate with American Indian tribes and gain insight on the best approaches to disseminate information about the Tobacco Control Act to Indian tribes and to tobacco retailers located on tribal lands.

[52] FDA also conducts investigations where free smokeless samples are distributed. Since beginning these investigations in fiscal year 2012, FDA had conducted 23 investigations as of March 31, 2014.

[53] Department of Health and Human Services, Food and Drug Administration, *Report to Congress: Progress and Effectiveness of the Implementation of the Family Smoking Prevention and Tobacco Control Act* (Silver Spring, Md.: Sept. 27, 2013). FDA has not established tobacco product manufacturing practices for tobacco manufacturers. FDA officials said they plan to do so.

[54] As of April 29, 2014, FDA reported there were 104 registered manufacturing facilities.

[55] Imported tobacco products must conform to the same regulatory requirements as domestic tobacco products with the following exception: foreign firms are not required to register their facility and to list their tobacco products.

[56] More than 650 determinations were related to an SE submission and more than 700 determinations were made in a stand-alone grandfathered review.

[57] In February 2014, FDA issued draft guidance stating that FDA does not intend to take enforcement action for 30 days on previously purchased products that a retailer has in its inventory. Department of Health and Human Services, Food and Drug Administration, Center for Tobacco Products, *Guidance for Industry and Tobacco Retailers: Enforcement Policy for Certain (Provisional) Tobacco Products that FDA Finds Not Substantially Equivalent (Draft Guidance),* accessed March 14, 2014, http://www.fda.gov/downloads/TobaccoProducts/GuidanceComplianceRegulatoryInformation/UCM386629.pdf.

[58] For more information on these surveillance activities, see Department of Health and Human Services, Food and Drug Administration, *Progress and Effectiveness of the Implementation of the Tobacco Control Act.*

[59] The Tobacco Control Act requires any smokeless tobacco product imported, sold, or distributed in the United States to have a product package label that includes one of the following required statements, “WARNING: This product can cause mouth cancer;” “WARNING: This product can cause gum disease and tooth loss;” “WARNING: This product is not a safe alternative to cigarettes;” “WARNING: Smokeless tobacco is addictive.” § 204, 123 Stat. at 1846 (codified at 15 U.S.C. § 4402(a)). The act also imposes specific requirements for the display of the warning label, including placement on the package and the type, size, and color of font used on the label. The act also includes requirements for advertisements of smokeless tobacco products, including the amount of space a warning must comprise and the language in which the advertisement appears.

[60] GAO-13-723, 27.

[61] OS staff is responsible for the regulatory science activities carried out by CTP, including building a product research base, conducting product reviews, and providing support for regulations and guidance.

[62] According to HHS, CTP has begun incorporating messages about the chemicals in tobacco products and specific HPHCs into its ongoing tobacco prevention campaign targeting at-risk youth, and additional messages may be incorporated into future public education campaigns currently in development.

[63] Among other things, CTP conducted and funded research on the initiation, use, perception, and toxicity of cigars, e-cigarettes, and other unregulated tobacco products.

[64] FDA issued the proposed rule on April 25, 2014. Comments on the proposed rule are due to FDA within 75 days, or July 9, 2014. 79 Fed. Reg. 23,142 (Apr. 25, 2014).

[65] The Tobacco Control Act does not mandate a time frame for CTP’s review of new tobacco product submissions with the exception of PMTA submissions. For PMTA submissions, the act requires CTP to issue an order stating whether the product may be marketed as promptly as possible, but not later than 180 days after FDA’s receipt of a submission.

[66] GAO-13-723.

[67] According to FDA, the time before October 1, 2014, will be used to develop tracking systems for monitoring progress in meeting the performance goals. See Department of Health and Human Services, Food and Drug Administration, "Establishing Four Performance Measures," accessed April 21, 2014, http://www.fda.gov/TobaccoProducts/NewsEvents/ucm393894.htm. FDA officials indicated that submissions for any newly deemed tobacco products received in fiscal years 2015 through 2018 would not be subject to the performance measures and time frames established on April 18, 2014.

[68] CTP prioritized its review of regular SE submissions over provisional SE submissions, and the agency made its first decisions on a regular SE submission in June 2013—about 8 months prior to its first decision on a provisional SE submission, which occurred in February 2014. Furthermore, CTP had completed the review process for seven times as many regular SE submissions (30 decisions) than provisional SE submissions (4 decisions) as of March 31, 2014.

In: Tobacco Products
Editor: Jared Hart

ISBN: 978-1-63463-183-9

Chapter 2

FDA FINAL RULE RESTRICTING THE SALE AND DISTRIBUTION OF CIGARETTES AND SMOKELESS TOBACCO*

C. Stephen Redhead and Jane M. Smith

SUMMARY

On March 19, 2010, the Food and Drug Administration (FDA) reissued a 1996 final rule aimed at reducing underage smoking and use of smokeless tobacco products (e.g., snuff, chewing tobacco). The agency's rulemaking was mandated by the Family Smoking Prevention and Tobacco Control Act, which was enacted last year in response to a 2000 decision by the Supreme Court holding that FDA lacked the statutory authority to regulate tobacco products. The Family Smoking Prevention and Tobacco Control Act (P.L. 111-31) expressly gives FDA broad statutory authority under the Federal Food, Drug, and Cosmetic Act (FFDCA) to regulate the manufacture, distribution, advertising, sale, and use of cigarettes and other tobacco products.

The new FDA tobacco rule builds on the youth access, marketing, and advertising restrictions that the tobacco companies agreed to as part of the 1998 Master Settlement Agreement, which settled lawsuits filed by the states to recover the public health costs of tobacco-related illness. Among

* This is an edited, reformatted and augmented version of a Congressional Research Service publication R41304, prepared for Members and Committees of Congress, dated May 2, 2013.

its provisions, the rule prohibits the sale of tobacco products to any person under age 18; requires retailers to verify a purchaser's age by photo ID; restricts the sale of tobacco products through vending machines and self-service displays to adult-only facilities; limits tobacco advertising in publications to which children and adolescents are exposed to a black-on-white, text-only format; prohibits the sale of tobacco brand-identified promotional items such as caps and T-shirts; and prohibits brand-name sponsorship of sporting and other cultural events. The rule became effective on June 22, 2010.

The original 1996 rule included a ban on outdoor cigarette and smokeless tobacco advertising (e.g., billboards, posters) within 1,000 feet of schools and playgrounds. The reissued rule does not incorporate such a ban. In *Lorillard Tobacco Co. v. Reilly* (2001), the U.S. Supreme Court struck down a similar outdoor advertising ban in Massachusetts, arguing that it violated the First Amendment protection of commercial speech. FDA has reserved a section in the reissued rule for future rulemaking on outdoor advertising restrictions. In a separate advanced notice of proposed rulemaking, the agency has requested public comment on this issue and offered several options for more narrowly tailored outdoor advertising restrictions that the agency believes would not violate the First Amendment.

In August 2009, several tobacco companies filed a federal lawsuit against FDA claiming that the Family Smoking Prevention and Tobacco Control Act violates their constitutional right to commercial free speech. On March 19, 2012, the U.S. Court of Appeals for the Sixth Circuit upheld the district court's decision striking down the tobacco rule's provision that limits advertising in publications with significant youth readership to a black-on-white, text-only format.

INTRODUCTION

On March 19, 2010, the Food and Drug Administration (FDA) reissued a 1996 final rule aimed at reducing underage smoking and use of smokeless tobacco products (e.g., snuff, chewing tobacco).[1] The agency's rulemaking was mandated by the Family Smoking Prevention and Tobacco Control Act (FSPTCA), which was enacted in 2009 after the Supreme Court, in a 2000 case entitled *FDA v. Brown & Williamson Tobacco Corp.*, determined that FDA lacked statutory authority to regulate tobacco products.[2] The new law expressly amends the Federal Food, Drug, and Cosmetic Act (FFDCA)[3] to give FDA broad statutory authority to regulate the manufacture, distribution, advertising, sale, and use of cigarettes and other tobacco products.

The FDA tobacco rule limits underage access to cigarettes and smokeless tobacco, and places new restrictions on the advertising and marketing of tobacco products. Among its provisions, the rule prohibits the sale of tobacco products to any person under age 18; requires retailers to verify a purchaser's age by photo ID; restricts the sale of tobacco products through vending machines and self-service displays; limits tobacco advertising in publications to which children and adolescents are exposed to a black-on-white, text-only format; prohibits the sale of tobacco brand-identified promotional items such as caps and T-shirts; and prohibits brand-name sponsorship of sporting and other cultural events. The rule took effect on June 22, 2010.

This report discusses FDA's initial failed attempt at regulating tobacco products under the then existing provisions of the FFDCA, summarizes FDA's current tobacco rule—reissued pursuant to statutory authority granted under the FSPTCA, and compares the reissued rule's provisions to the youth access, advertising, and marketing restrictions that went into effect pursuant to the 1998 Master Settlement Agreement between the states and the tobacco companies. The report then discusses the First Amendment implications of the rule's advertising restrictions and includes an analysis of the U.S. Supreme Court's decision in *Lorillard Tobacco Co. v. Reilly*, which struck down a Massachusetts law restricting outdoor tobacco advertising, and a recent federal court of appeals ruling against FDA.

FDA's Initial Attempt to Regulate Tobacco Products

Recognizing the health hazards of smoking, FDA first attempted to regulate tobacco products in the 1990s as a "drug or device" under the then existing provisions of the Federal Food, Drug, and Cosmetic Act (FFDCA). Accordingly, FDA published a final rule on August 28, 1996, aimed at reducing underage smoking and use of smokeless tobacco products.[4] The FDA rule included three sets of provisions: restrictions on the sale and distribution of tobacco products to minors, limits on tobacco-product marketing and advertising, and new labeling requirements for packaging and advertising. The agency said that the purpose of the rule was to reduce the easy access to tobacco products by minors. It also hoped to reduce the amount of positive advertising imagery used by manufacturers to make their products appealing to minors. While the rule did not directly address adult tobacco use, FDA argued that over time it would help reduce adult tobacco consumption. Data from the National Survey on Drug Use and Health indicate that the vast majority of smokers take up the habit as teenagers. Thus, reducing the number of new teenage smokers, who were needed to replace adult smokers who quit or die, was expected to lower overall tobacco consumption in the future.

Agency Assertion of Jurisdiction over Tobacco Products

The FDA initially asserted regulatory jurisdiction over cigarettes and smokeless tobacco under the FFDCA by concluding that nicotine was a "drug" and that cigarettes and smokeless tobacco were a drug-delivery "device" as defined by the act. The statute defines a drug, in relevant part, as "articles (other than food) *intended* to affect the structure or any function of the body."[5] In its rulemaking, the FDA drew on the extensive scientific literature documenting nicotine's pharmacologic effects on the body, including satisfaction of addiction, stimulation, and sedation. The agency also concluded that cigarettes and smokeless tobacco are devices that deliver nicotine into the body. As with drugs, the FFDCA's definition of medical devices includes articles that are intended by the manufacturer to affect the structure and function of the body.[6] Unlike a drug, however, a device is defined, in part, as an article "which does not achieve its primary intended purpose through chemical action."[7]

Having made the determination that tobacco products fell under the statutory definitions of drugs and devices, the FDA further concluded that these products were combination products because they have both a drug and a device components. Under the FFDCA, the FDA is authorized to regulate products that "constitute a combination of a drug, device, or biologic product."[8] The agency interpreted this provision as giving it the discretion to regulate combination products as drugs, as devices, or as biologic products.[9] In its final rule, the FDA chose to regulate tobacco products under the device provisions of the FFDCA because they offered the agency greater regulatory flexibility than did the drug provisions of the act.[10]

Under the FFDCA, drug and device manufacturers must demonstrate that their products are both safe and effective in order to gain FDA marketing approval.[11] The safety and effectiveness standard poses a difficult challenge for regulating tobacco products, which are manifestly unsafe when used as intended. Critics of FDA's 1996 rule argued that in asserting regulatory authority over tobacco products, the agency would have no choice but to ban them because of their harmful and addictive effects. In commenting on the rule, the FDA conceded that tobacco products are "unsafe" as that term is generally understood, but concluded that banning tobacco products was not a realistic option because the health care system would be overwhelmed by more than 40 million nicotine addicts seeking assistance for withdrawal symptoms. Moreover, the agency argued, banning cigarettes would create an enormous black market, which might lead to the use of unregulated and potentially even more harmful products.

The FFDCA's device authorities present a range of mandatory controls that apply to devices and their manufacturers including labeling and recordkeeping requirements, registration and inspection, and good manufacturing practices. In addition to mandatory controls, the FFDCA contains various discretionary provisions that apply to devices under certain circumstances. The FDA predicated its authority to regulate tobacco products on one such provision regarding restricted devices. The act's restricted device provision states, in relevant part, that "[t]he Secretary may by regulation require that a device be restricted to sale, distribution, or use ... upon such other conditions as the Secretary may prescribe in such regulation, if, *because of its potentiality for harmful effect or the collateral measures necessary for its use*, the Secretary determines that there cannot otherwise be reasonable assurance of its safety and effectiveness."[12]

In the final tobacco rule, the FDA relied on the FFDCA's restricted device provision when it concluded that, because of the harmful effects of cigarette and smokeless tobacco and in the absence of a reasonable assurance of the safety and effectiveness of such products, it needed to implement additional restrictions on tobacco access and advertising in order to prevent new users from becoming addicted.[13]

Legal Challenge to the 1996 Rule

Following the release of the 1996 tobacco rule, tobacco companies filed a lawsuit against the FDA and sought summary judgment on the grounds that the agency lacked the authority to regulate tobacco products when such products are marketed and sold without explicit claims of therapeutic benefit. The lawsuit further charged that the FDA exceeded its statutory authority because the FFDCA did not authorize the FDA to regulate tobacco products as drugs or devices.[14] Finally, the companies argued that the rule's advertising restrictions, which limited most advertisements to a black-on-white text-only format, violated the First Amendment protection of commercial speech.

In a 2000 case entitled *FDA v. Brown & Williamson Tobacco Corp.*, the U.S. Supreme Court, in a 5-4 decision written by Justice Sandra Day O'Connor, affirmed that the FDA did not have the authority to regulate tobacco products as drug-delivery devices.[15] Although the majority opinion acknowledged the public health threat posed by tobacco use, the Court concluded that "Congress has clearly precluded the FDA from asserting jurisdiction to regulate tobacco products. Such authority is inconsistent with the intent that Congress has expressed in the [FFDCA's] overall regulatory scheme and in the tobacco-specific legislation that it has enacted subsequent to the [FFDCA]."[16]

In reaching its decision, the Court examined the FDA tobacco rule in light of the precedents that govern cases involving an agency's construction of a statute that it administers. As part of such a review, the Court must determine whether an agency's interpretation of its statute is entitled to deference and presents a reasonable or permissible construction of the law. *Chevron U.S.A., Inc. v. Natural Resources Defense Council, Inc.* is the leading case on judicial review of agency interpretations of statutes.[17] This case involved the Environmental Protection Agency's rules regulating emissions under the Clean Air Act. In *Chevron*, the Court enunciated a two-step test for judicial review of an agency's interpretation of its statute: (1) has Congress spoken directly to the precise question at issue? and (2) if Congress has not done so and the statute is silent or ambiguous with respect to the specific issue, is the agency's answer based on a permissible construction of the statute?[18]

Under *Chevron* step one, if Congress has spoken directly to the question at issue, then *Chevron* deference is not due and the court "must give effect to the unambiguously expressed intent of Congress."[19] In this case, the Court examined both the FFDCA and other tobacco-related statutes, ultimately concluding that Congress had clearly intended to preclude the FDA from regulating tobacco. As a result, the Court did not need to reach step two of *Chevron*. In reaching its decision, the court relied on a number of factors. First, the Court found that, because tobacco is a dangerous product and because the FFDCA prohibits the marketing of products that have not been found to be safe and effective, the statute would require the FDA to ban tobacco products if the agency did indeed have jurisdiction over such products. Such a ban, argued the Court, would plainly contradict the congressional intent reflected in the enactment of several pieces of legislation that clearly contemplate the continued marketing of tobacco products.[20] Thus, the Court held that Congress had clearly "intended to exclude tobacco products from the FDA's jurisdiction."[21]

In addition, the Court found that the FDA had repeatedly denied that it had jurisdiction over tobacco and that Congress had repeatedly rejected bills that would have granted the agency such authority.[22] Instead, Congress had demonstrated its intent to create a distinct regulatory scheme for tobacco by enacting other tobacco-related regulatory statutes, such as the Federal Cigarette Labeling and Advertising Act and the Comprehensive Smokeless Tobacco Health Education Act.[23] The Court cited these tobacco-related statutes as additional evidence in support of its conclusion that Congress had intended to preclude the FDA from regulating tobacco.[24]

Writing in dissent, Justice Stephen Breyer argued that cigarettes and other tobacco products clearly fall within the plain meaning of the statutory definition of drugs and devices because such products are intended to affect the structure and function of the body. In addition, the dissent argued that the purpose of the FFDCA—to protect the public health—also supported the conclusion that the FDA was authorized to regulate tobacco products. For these reasons, the dissent would have upheld the FDA's jurisdiction over such products.[25]

FAMILY SMOKING PREVENTION AND TOBACCO CONTROL ACT

Following *Brown & Williamson*, it was evident that the FDA could not regulate tobacco products unless Congress provided the agency with the express statutory authority to do so. To that end, the Family Smoking Prevention and Tobacco Control Act (H.R. 4433, S. 2461) was first introduced in the 108th Congress by Representatives Tom Davis and Henry Waxman and Senators Mike DeWine and Ted Kennedy to grant FDA statutory authority over tobacco products. The legislation was the product of months of negotiations in which lawmakers sought to balance the competing interests of public health groups and the tobacco industry. The Senate added S. 2461 as an amendment to a corporate tax package,[26] but the language was subsequently removed in conference by House conferees.

The Family Smoking Prevention and Tobacco Control Act was reintroduced in the 109th Congress (H.R. 1376, S. 666) and again in the 110th Congress (H.R. 1108, S. 625), during which it was approved by committees in both the House and Senate. The House passed H.R. 1108 in July 2008, but no further legislative action was taken during the 110th Congress. Reintroduced in the 111th Congress, the Family Smoking Prevention and Tobacco Control Act (H.R. 1256) passed the House on April 2, 2009. The Senate passed a slightly different version of the legislation (S. 982) on June 11, 2009, which the House agreed to the following day. The Family Smoking Prevention and Tobacco Control Act (FSPTCA) was signed into law on June 22, 2009 (P.L. 111-31).

The FSPTCA amended the FFDCA by granting FDA authority over the regulation of tobacco products based on a public health standard rather than the safety and effectiveness standard by which the FDA regulates pharmaceutical drugs and medical devices. The new law gives FDA the authority to develop regulations restricting the sale, distribution, advertising, and promotion of tobacco products. Any proposed regulation must meet the new public health standard. That standard requires FDA to demonstrate that the proposal is appropriate for the protection of the public health, taking into account the risks and benefits to the population as a whole, including users and nonusers of tobacco products. In addition, FDA has the authority to require changes in the design and characteristics of current and future tobacco products, such as the reduction or elimination of harmful ingredients and additives. Again, the agency must show that any such proposal is appropriate for protecting public health, based on a consideration of the risks and benefits to the population as a whole.

Under the FSPTCA, manufacturers must obtain FDA approval in order to market a new tobacco product. The same public health standard applies to such applications. However, the law provides two exceptions to the requirement that manufacturers obtain premarket approval for new products: (1) the manufacturer makes a claim and FDA, upon review, agrees that the new product is substantially equivalent to a product already on the market, or (2) the new product is determined to be a "minor modification" of an existing product.[27] For the first 21 months after enactment (i.e., until March 22, 2011), manufacturers are permitted to introduce and market a new product for which a substantial equivalence claim has been submitted, provided FDA has not reviewed and rejected the claim.[28]

The FSPTCA prohibits the use of descriptors such as "light" and "mild."[29] Manufacturers seeking to market a tobacco product for which they wish to make a reduced-risk claim, explicitly or implicitly, must provide evidence substantiating that claim and meet additional requirements in order to obtain FDA approval to market the product.[30] The law requires a number of other important changes in the labeling, advertising, and marketing of cigarettes and smokeless tobacco products. Beginning on June 22, 2010, more explicit and conspicuous health warnings will start to appear on smokeless tobacco product labels and advertising.[31] New health warnings on cigarette labeling and advertising will appear at a later date. FDA also has the authority to revise the size and content of the warnings, if it determines that such changes would promote a greater public understanding of the health risks of tobacco use.[32]

FDA Rule on Cigarettes and Smokeless Tobacco

The FSPTCA also required FDA to reissue a modified version of the 1996 tobacco rule that the Supreme Court struck down in *Brown & Williamson.*

Summary of Provisions

The reissued tobacco rule's provisions restricting the sale, advertising, and marketing of cigarettes and smokeless tobacco are summarized in the box below.[33] Generally, each manufacturer, distributor, and retailer is responsible for ensuring that the tobacco products it manufactures, labels, advertises, distributes, or sells comply with these provisions.[34] Retailers, for example, must ensure that all self-service displays and advertising located within their establishments that do not comply with the rule's provisions are removed or brought into compliance.[35]

Summary of FDA Final Rule Restricting the Sale and Distribution of Cigarettes and Smokeless Tobacco (21 C.F.R. Part 1140)

Youth Access Restrictions

- Prohibits the sale of cigarettes or smokeless tobacco to persons under age 18.
- Requires retailers to check photo ID to verify age of purchasers under age 27.
- Requires that retail sales be conducted in a direct, face-to-face exchange, with the exception of vending machine sales and self-service displays as described below.

- Permits tobacco-product vending machines and self-service displays but only in facilities where individuals under age 18 are not permitted to enter at any time.
- Prohibits the sale or distribution of individual cigarettes or packages containing fewer than 20 cigarettes, except in vending machines located in facilities where individuals under age 18 are not permitted to enter at any time.
- Prohibits free samples of cigarettes; permits free samples of smokeless tobacco in qualified adult-only facilities, as defined.

Marketing and Advertising Restrictions

- Limits advertising in publications with significant youth readership to a black-on-white, text-only format.[a]
- Limits advertising in audio format to words with no music or sound effects; limits advertising in video format to static, black-on-white text.
- Prohibits the marketing, licensing, distribution, or sale of all non-tobacco items and services identified with a cigarette or smokeless tobacco brand name (e.g., promotional T-shirts and caps).
- Prohibits gifts, credits, and coupons linked to the purchase of tobacco products.
- Prohibits brand-name sponsorship of sporting and other cultural events, but permits corporate-name sponsorship of such events.
- Prohibits the use of a non-tobacco trade or brand name as a tobacco product trade or brand name, unless that tobacco product trade or brand name was on both a tobacco product and a non-tobacco product sold in the United States on Jan. 1, 1995.

a. Due to the ruling by the U.S. District Court for the Western District of Kentucky in *Commonwealth Brands v. U.S.*, discussed *infra*, FDA has stated it does not intend to commence enforcement actions under this provision while litigation is pending.

The FSPTCA instructed FDA to reissue the 1996 rule as a final rule with the following specified exceptions. First, the agency was instructed to drop the original rule's labeling provisions that would have required cigarette and smokeless tobacco packaging and advertising to include the statement "Nicotine Delivery Device for Persons 18 and Older."[36] The FSPTCA gives FDA new authority to regulate tobacco product labeling and advertising. Second, FDA was required to replace the definitions of "cigarettes," "cigarette tobacco," and "smokeless tobacco" as they appeared in the original rule with the definitions of those terms included in the FSPTCA.[37] Third, the agency was directed to modify the provision in the original rule that would have prohibited the distribution of free samples of cigarettes or smokeless tobacco with language in the FSPTCA that permits the distribution of free smokeless tobacco samples in "qualified adult-only facilities," as defined.[38]

Finally, the FSPTCA instructed FDA to consider modifications to the original rule's ban on outdoor cigarette and smokeless tobacco advertising (e.g., billboards, posters) within 1,000 feet of schools and playgrounds so as to address First Amendment case law, including the 2001 U.S. Supreme Court decision in *Lorillard Tobacco Co. v. Reilly*.[39] In *Lorillard*, discussed in more detail *infra*, the Court struck down a Massachusetts state ban on outdoor tobacco advertising within 1,000 feet of any school or playground, holding that it violated the First Amendment protection of commercial speech. The reissued final rule does not include the outdoor advertising ban. FDA has instead reserved a section in the rule for future rulemaking on outdoor advertising restrictions. In a separate advanced notice of proposed rulemaking, the agency has requested public comment on this issue and offered several options for more narrowly tailored outdoor advertising restrictions that it believes would not violate the First Amendment.[40] To date, the FDA has not published a Notice of Proposed Rulemaking.

Retail establishments are responsible for providing training to their employees on the new regulations. FDA is planning to publish guidance to assist retailers in complying with the new regulations. The agency intends to enforce retailer compliance with the rule through inspections. The FSPTCA requires the agency to contract with states to inspect retail establishments.[41] FDA has indicated that it will enter into these contracts on a rolling basis, but that in the interim it intends to conduct its own inspections and take enforcement action when appropriate. FDA has a variety of enforcement tools to address retailer noncompliance, including civil monetary penalties, warning letters, injunctions, and/or criminal prosecution. Retailers who violate the regulations may also be in violation of state law and subject to a variety of state remedies.[42]

In August 2009, several tobacco companies filed a federal lawsuit against FDA claiming that the FSPTCA violated their constitutional right to commercial free speech. On January 5, 2010, a federal district court judge struck down the tobacco rule's provision that limits advertising in publications with significant youth readership to a black-on-white text-only format. That ruling, which FDA is expected to appeal, is discussed in more detail below.

Comparison of FDA Rule with the Master Settlement Agreement

The FDA rule builds on the youth access, marketing, and advertising restrictions that the tobacco companies agreed to as part of the 1998 Master Settlement Agreement (MSA). Attorneys general from 46 states, the District of Columbia (DC), and the five U.S. territories signed the MSA with the major cigarette companies to settle lawsuits filed by the states to recover the public health costs of treating smokers. The remaining four states (Florida, Minnesota, Mississippi, and Texas) reached comparable individual settlements with the companies. The MSA committed the tobacco companies to pay the states approximately $200 billion over the first 25 years, subject to inflation and other adjustments, with payments to continue in perpetuity.[43] In addition, the MSA included the following restrictions on youth access, marketing, and advertising, all of which remain in effect (unless noted otherwise).

Summary of the Tobacco Master Settlement Agreement (MSA) Restrictions on Youth Access, Marketing and Advertising

Youth Access Restrictions

- Limits free samples to adult-only facilities.
- Prohibits packages containing fewer than 20 cigarettes. (Note: This provision expired at the end of 2001.)

Marketing and Advertising Restriction

- Prohibits the use of cartoon images in advertising.
- Prohibits industry payments to promote tobacco products in movies, TV shows, live performances, commercial films and videos, or video games, unless the audience or viewers are in an adult-only facility.
- Prohibits non-tobacco merchandise (e.g., caps, T-shirts) with tobacco brand-name logos, except at brand-name sponsored events.
- Prohibits gifts of non-tobacco items to youth in exchange for the purchase of tobacco products.
- Permits corporate-name sponsorship of sporting and cultural events and limits each company to brand-name sponsorship of one event per year (which may not include concerts, team sports, events with a significant youth audience, or events with underage contestants).

- Prohibits public transit advertising, and prohibits outdoor billboard advertising in arenas, stadiums, shopping malls, and arcades. Permits such advertising at brand-name sponsored events.
- Permits poster-sized advertising (up to 14 sq. ft.) on or outside retail establishments.

The FDA rule expands the MSA youth access restrictions by restoring the 20-cigarette minimum pack size and banning free samples of cigarettes entirely. In addition, the rule places new restrictions on retailers—requiring photo identification of persons under age 28 and face-to-face retail exchanges—and limits vending machine sales to adult-only locations. Comparable provisions were not included in the MSA.

Regarding tobacco product marketing and advertising, the FDA rule goes beyond the MSA in banning all brand-name sponsorship of sporting and other cultural events. And, unlike the MSA, the rule places new restrictions on tobacco labeling and advertising in publications with a significant youth readership and in audio and video advertisements. However, FDA has decided not to include a ban on all outdoor tobacco advertising within 1,000 feet of a school or playground. As discussed in more detail in the next section of this report, the agency is seeking public comment on more narrowly tailored outdoor advertising restrictions.

FIRST AMENDMENT CHALLENGES TO THE TOBACCO RULE

The FDA's reissued tobacco rule includes marketing and advertising restrictions that raise constitutional questions as to the resulting burden placed on commercial speech.[44] As authorized by the FSPTCA, FDA is also considering modifications to a ban on outdoor advertising within 1,000 feet of a school or playground in light of First Amendment case law.[45] The U.S. Supreme Court has issued a series of decisions striking down government restrictions on certain types of commercial speech, including tobacco product advertising.[46] These cases are instructive and form the basis for a federal court's analysis of the early legal challenges to the reissued tobacco rule.

Legal Overview of Restrictions on Tobacco Advertising and Marketing

In *Central Hudson Gas & Electric Corp. v. Public Service Commission*, the U.S. Supreme Court established a four-part test for deciding the constitutionality of commercial speech regulation.[47] First, in order to be protected by the First Amendment, the commercial speech must concern lawful activity and not be false or misleading. Second, the government must demonstrate that by restricting such speech, it is seeking to further a substantial government interest. Third, the restrictions must directly advance that interest. Fourth, there has to be a reasonable fit between the type of restrictions imposed and the government's objectives; in other words, the regulation cannot be "more extensive than is necessary to service that interest."[48]

As discussed previously, the FSPTCA required FDA to reissue most of the agency's 1996 tobacco rule as a final rule, with some additional language. In developing the 1996 tobacco rule, FDA created a set of advertising restrictions aimed at reducing underage smoking and smokeless tobacco use that it hoped would withstand a constitutional challenge. However, whether the FDA's 1996 rule—which included the restrictions on outdoor advertising, color graphics, and sponsorships—would have passed the *Central Hudson* test was a question never reached by the Supreme Court. In *FDA v. Brown & Williamson*, the Court instead confined itself to the more fundamental issue of agency authority to regulate tobacco at all. The Court did not address the constitutionality of the rule's marketing restrictions.

Although the Supreme Court did not reach the merits of the 1996 FDA rule's advertising restrictions in *Brown & Williamson*, the Court has considered similar state restrictions on tobacco product advertising. In the 2001 case, *Lorillard Tobacco Co. v. Reilly*, the Court found a number of Massachusetts state regulations restricting outdoor and point-of-sale advertising for cigars and smokeless tobacco products to be unconstitutional.[49] The Court determined that the regulations restricted speech more than was reasonable to advance the state's interest in reducing underage (i.e., illegal) use of tobacco products and, thus, failed to meet the fourth part of the *Central Hudson* test.[50]

One of the invalidated restrictions was an outdoor advertising provision with nearly identical language to the 1996 FDA tobacco rule's prohibition on outdoor tobacco advertisements within 1,000 feet of a school or playground.[51] Such a restriction, in conjunction with other zoning restrictions, reasoned the

Court, "would constitute a nearly complete ban on the communication of truthful information about smokeless tobacco and cigars to adult consumers."[52] The Court found that the restrictions on outdoor advertising of cigars and smokeless tobacco were too broad in that they prohibited advertising "in a substantial portion of the major metropolitan areas of Massachusetts," included oral communications, and imposed burdens on retailers with limited advertising budgets.[53] The Court also upheld challenges by smokeless tobacco and cigar companies to the outdoor advertising restrictions on the grounds that adults have a right to information and the tobacco industry has a right to communicate truthful speech on legal products.[54]

The Court's reasoning in *Lorillard* is likely to be instructive for any future consideration of the FDA's outdoor advertising provisions. In defending the state regulation, the Massachusetts Attorney General relied to a substantial degree on studies and evidence associated with the advertising restrictions in the FDA's 1996 rule.[55] Although the Court determined that Massachusetts had presented sufficient evidence to satisfy the first three prongs of the *Central Hudson* test, the outdoor advertising regulations were found to be too broad to meet the fourth requirement—that is, that the regulation not be "more extensive than is necessary."[56]

The Court's key finding in the *Lorillard* case was that Massachusetts had not engaged in a "careful calculation" of the costs of the advertising regulation, nor did the state "seem to consider the impact of the 1,000-foot restriction on commercial speech in major metropolitan areas."[57] Rather, the Attorney General simply imposed a 1,000 foot restriction that was identical to the FDA's restriction in the 1996 rule. The Court accepted the lower court's finding that the broad restriction would prohibit advertising in 87%-91% of the greater Boston metropolitan area.[58] Such an extensive ban, reasoned the Court, "would constitute nearly a complete ban on the communication of truthful information about smokeless tobacco and cigars to adult consumers" and therefore did not "demonstrate a careful calculation of the speech interests involved."[59] The Court also criticized the fact that the regulation constituted a ban on signs of any size, prevented retailers from communicating legitimate commercial messages to passersby, and applied to indoor communications that could be seen from the outside.[60] In short, Massachusetts had failed to demonstrate that the regulation was sufficiently tailored to achieving the state's substantial interest in preventing minors' access to tobacco.[61]

Because Massachusetts relied greatly on studies and evidence supporting the FDA's proposed 1996 outdoor advertising regulation, the Court did, in dicta, reference the FDA rule. In discussing the geographical implications of

Massachusetts' 1,000-foot ban, the Court simply noted that "the FDA's regulations would have had widely disparate effects nationwide."[62] The Court also suggested that a "uniform ... geographical limitation," without taking account of the differences between rural, suburban, and urban communities, "demonstrates a lack of tailoring."[63] FDA received comments in response to the 1996 rule that identified this very issue. In the FDA's 1996 final rule, the agency took note of comments that focused on the impact of the rule in major metropolitan areas, including a survey that "showed that outdoor tobacco advertising would be prohibited in 94 percent and 78 percent of the respective land mass of Manhattan and Boston under the [1,000-foot] proposal."[64] However, the FDA attributed "the possibility that its restrictions effectively outlaw outdoor advertising in most urban areas" to population density in cities.[65] The agency then stated that its intent in establishing the 1,000-foot restriction was "to restrict the accessible and intrusive communications of information about cigarettes and smokeless tobacco to children and adolescents at school and at play."[66] The rule explained that the FDA "considered the cost of its [1,000-foot] restriction but conclude[d] that a narrower restriction would not adequately advance its purpose of protecting young people from unavoidable advertising."[67]

Early Legal Challenges to the Reissued Tobacco Rule

Several tobacco companies were quick to challenge the advertising and marketing provisions of the reissued tobacco rule, citing *Lorillard* and arguing that the restrictions violated the free speech protections of the First Amendment. The U.S. Court of Appeals for the Sixth Circuit, the first appellate court to consider the validity of the new rule, released a "mixed ruling" on March 19, 2012, striking down some provisions of the regulation while upholding others.[68]

In *Discount Tobacco City and Lottery v. United States*, the court of appeals held that the FSPTCA's prohibition on color and graphical advertising violated the tobacco company's First Amendment free speech rights.[69] The court treated the regulation as a blanket ban of color and imagery in advertising.[70] Noting that such blanket bans are disfavored, the court wrote that "[i]nstead of instituting a blanket restriction on color and graphics in tobacco advertising, the government may instead restrict only the speech necessary to effect its purposes."[71] Quoting the Supreme Court's opinion in *Lorillard*, the court stated, "To the extent that studies have identified particular advertising promotion practices that appeal to youth, tailoring would involve targeting those practices while permitting others."[72] Therefore, under the court's opinion, the government may ban advertising directed at youth, but it may not ban advertising for adults because "'so long as the sale and use of tobacco is lawful for adults, the tobacco industry has a protected interest in communicating information about its products and adult customers have an interest in receiving that information.'"[73] Therefore, the court of appeals concluded that the ban on color graphics and text failed the fourth prong of the *Central Hudson* test because it was more extensive than necessary.[74]

The court largely upheld the remaining restrictions on tobacco advertising and marketing. The court upheld the provisions prohibiting the distribution of free samples[75] and branded non-tobacco products,[76] and brand-name sponsorship of events.[77] However, it struck down the rule's ban on so-called "continuity programs," which allow consumers to redeem proofs of purchase for merchandise.[78]

The district court did not reach the merits of the tobacco rule's outdoor advertising restrictions, and the cigarette companies did not appeal that portion of the decision. While the district court implied that a ban on outdoor advertising within 1,000 feet of a school or playground, such as the prohibition found in the original 1996 rule, was "undoubtedly" unconstitutional under *Lorillard*, the court held that an immediate challenge to the outdoor advertising ban was not yet ripe for review.[79] Under the FSPTCA, Congress mandated that the FDA "include such modifications" to the outdoor advertising restriction as deemed appropriate "in light of governing First Amendment case law."[80] The FDA has yet to issue any such modifications. Accordingly, a challenge to the restriction is not yet ripe for judicial consideration.

The validity of the reissued tobacco rule's outdoor advertising restrictions will likely hinge on the nature of the modifications issued by the FDA. Analyzing the restriction on outdoor advertising in the context of *Central Hudson*, *Lorillard*, and *Discount Tobacco*, it does not appear that an unconditional or unaltered restriction on advertisements within 1,000 feet of a school or playground would survive the fourth step of the *Central Hudson* test (i.e., that the regulation cannot be "more extensive than is necessary" to serve the substantial government interest).[81] In *Lorillard*, for example, the Court explained that a "careful calculation of the costs of a speech regulation does not mean that a State must demonstrate that there is no incursion on legitimate speech interests, but a speech regulation cannot unduly impinge on the speaker's ability to propose a commercial transaction and the adult listener's opportunity to obtain information about products."[82] Thus, any modification to the rule's outdoor advertising provision will need to carefully balance the FDA's substantial interest in protecting children from tobacco products with the tobacco companies' legitimate right to convey commercial information to adults.

Although the FSPTCA does not require the FDA to modify the outdoor advertising restrictions included in the 1996 rule,[83] the FDA appears to have determined that a more narrowly tailored restriction is advisable. The reissued final rule does not include the outdoor advertising ban. FDA has instead reserved a section in the rule for future rulemaking on outdoor advertising restrictions. In a separate advanced notice of proposed rulemaking that FDA published on the same day as the final rule, the agency requested comments, data, and research "pertaining to potential outdoor advertising restrictions for tobacco products that may have developed since ... 1996."[84] In addition, FDA announced that it was considering "several options" for altering the 1996 outdoor advertising provision, including limiting the outdoor advertising prohibition to only apply to billboards within 1,000 feet of elementary or secondary schools, or prohibiting "signs or collections of advertisements greater than 14 square feet at retail establishments located in close proximity to any elementary or secondary school (e.g., within 350 feet or approximately one city block)."[85] FDA also noted that it was considering creating a sliding scale regulatory scheme that prohibits advertisements of varying size in relation to the sign's proximity to an elementary or secondary school.

Given the legal restraints, some public health law experts believe that the U.S. Supreme Court in its decisions on the regulation of commercial speech has left public health authorities with limited room to craft tobacco advertising restrictions that meet both the third (effectiveness) and fourth (extensiveness) parts of the *Central Hudson* test.[86] On the one hand, tobacco advertising restrictions that are narrowly tailored may not provide clear evidence of effectiveness, thus failing the third part of *Central Hudson* test. On the other hand, more sweeping (and potentially effective) restrictions may be viewed as too extensive and not reasonably related to the government's asserted interest, thus failing the fourth part of the *Central Hudson* test.

End Notes

[1] Department of Health and Human Services, Food and Drug Administration, "Regulations Restricting the Sale and Distribution of Cigarettes and Smokeless Tobacco to Protect Children and Adolescents," 75 Federal Register 13225- 13232, March 19, 2010.

[2] P.L. 111-31; 123 Stat. 1776; 529 U.S. 120 (2000).

[3] 21 U.S.C. §§ 301 et seq.

[4] 61 Federal Register 44396-45318; 21 C.F.R. Parts 801, 803, 804, 807, 820, and 897.

[5] 21 U.S.C. § 321(g)(1)(C); FFDCA § 201(g)(1)(C) (emphasis added).

[6] 21 U.S.C. § 321(h)(3); FFDCA § 201(h)(3).

[7] 21 U.S.C. § 321(h); FFDCA § 201(h).

[8] 21 U.S.C. § 353(g); FFDCA § 503(g).

[9] 61 Federal Register 44396, 44400 (1996).

[10] Id. at 44403. In 2005, FDA published a final rule setting forth definitions and an algorithm the agency uses to assign combination products to an agency component for regulatory oversight. 69 Federal Register 49848 (2005).

[11] See CRS Report RL32826, The Medical Device Approval Process and Related Legislative Issues, by Erin D. Williams, available upon request.

[12] 21 U.S.C. § 360j(e); FFDCA § 520(e) (emphasis added).

[13] 61 Federal Register 44396, 44405.

[14] Coyne Beahm, Inc. v. FDA, 966 F. Supp. 1374 (M.D.N.C. 1997).

[15] FDA v. Brown & Williamson Tobacco Corp., 529 U.S. 120 (2000).

[16] Id. at 126.

[17] 467 U.S. 837 (1984).

[18] Id. at 842-43.

[19] Id. at 843.

[20] FDA v. Brown & Williamson Tobacco Corp., 529 U.S. 120, 134-43 (2000). Examples of such tobacco-related legislation include the Federal Cigarette Labeling and Advertising Act (P.L. 89-92, 15 U.S.C. §§ 1331 et seq.); the Public Health Cigarette Smoking Act of 1969 (P.L. 91-222, 15 U.S.C. §§ 1331 et seq.); the Comprehensive Smoking Education Act (P.L. 98-474, 15 U.S.C. §§ 1331 et seq.); the Comprehensive Smokeless Tobacco Health Education Act of 1986 (P.L. 99-252, 15 U.S.C. §§ 4401 et seq.); and the Alcohol, Drug Abuse, and Mental Health Administration Reorganization Act (P.L. 102-321, § 202, 42 U.S.C. § 300x-26).

[21] Brown & Williamson, 529 U.S. at 143.

[22] According to the tobacco companies, beginning in 1906 and as recently as 1993, Congress rejected any legislation designed to give the FDA jurisdiction over tobacco. See, First Amended Complaint for Declaratory and Injunctive Relief at 6-11, Coyne Beahm, Inc. v. FDA, 966 F. Supp. 1374 (M.D.N.C. 1997) (No. 2:95CV00591).

[23] These statutes, both of which are administered by the FTC, require health warnings on cigarette and smokeless tobacco packages and advertising, respectively.

[24] Brown & Williamson, 529 U.S. at 143-156.

[25] Id. at 161-64.

[26] American Jobs Creation Act of 2004, P.L. 108-357; 118 Stat. 1418.

[27] 21 U.S.C. § 387j.

[28] 21 U.S.C. § 387j

[29] 21 U.S.C. § 387k.

[30] 21 U.S.C. § 387k.

[31] As of 30 days after June 22, 2010 manufacturers may not introduce into interstate commerce any smokeless tobacco product, regardless of its date of manufacture, that does not bear the new health warnings.

[32] 15 U.S.C. § 1333; 15 U.S.C. § 4402.

[33] The FDA tobacco rule is codified in a new Part 1140 in Title 21 of the Code of Federal Regulations.

[34] 21 C.F.R. § 1140.10.

[35] 21 C.F.R. § 1140.14(e).

[36] FSPTCA § 102, P.L. 111-31.

[37] FSPTCA § 102, P.L. 111-31.

[38] FSPTCA § 102, P.L. 111-31.

[39] 533 U.S. 525 (2001); FSPTCA § 102, P.L. 111-31.

[40] Department of Health and Human Services, Food and Drug Administration, "Request for Comment on Implementation of the Family Smoking Prevention and Tobacco Control Act," 75 Federal Register 13241-13243, March 19, 2010.

[41] FSPTCA § 103(g), P.L. 111-31.

[42] FDA has more information about retailer compliance, inspection, and enforcement, at http://www.fda.gov/ TobaccoProducts/ProtectingKidsfromTobacco/RegsRestrictingSale/default.htm.

[43] A detailed analysis of the MSA is beyond the scope of this report. For more information on the MSA payment formula and adjustments, and the states' allocations of those funds, see U.S. Government Accountability Office, Tobacco Settlement: States' Allocations of Payments from Tobacco Companies for Fiscal Years 2000 through 2005, GAO-07-534T, February 27, 2007, http://www.gao.gov/new.items/d07534t.pdf.

[44] The tobacco rule implements a number of marketing and advertising restrictions, including (1) limiting tobacco labeling and advertising to black text on a white background in publications with a significant youth readership that does not meet the rule's definition of an adult population; and (2) prohibiting brand-name event sponsorship and brand-name merchandising. See, 21 C.F.R. § 1140.32(a) ("...any labeling or advertising for cigarettes or smokeless tobacco shall use only black text on a white background."). Except in facilities "where vending machines and self-service displays are permitted ... provided that the advertising is not visible from outside the facility and that it is affixed to a wall or fixture in the facility" or in an "adult publication." An adult publication is defined under 21 C.F.R. § 1140.32(a)(2) as:

a newspaper, magazine, periodical, or other publication: (i) Whose readers younger than 18 years of age constitute 15 percent or less of the total readership as measured by competent and reliable survey evidence; and (ii) That is read by fewer than 2 million persons younger than 18 years of age as measured by competent and reliable survey evidence.

See also, 21 C.F.R. § 1140.34(a) ("No manufacturer or distributor ... may market, license, distribute, sell ... any item (other than cigarettes or smokeless tobacco or roll-your-own paper) or service which bears the brand name ... logo, symbol ... or any other indicia of product identification identical or similar to ... those used for any brand of cigarettes or smokeless tobacco."). See also, 21 C.F.R. § 1140.34(c) ("No manufacturer, distributor, or retailer may sponsor or cause to be sponsored any athletic, musical, artistic, or other social or cultural event.... ").

[45] 21 U.S.C. § 387a-1.

[46] Ronald Beyer et al., "Tobacco Advertising in the United States: A Proposal for a Constitutionally Acceptable Form of Regulation," Journal of the American Medical Association, vol. 287, no. 22 (June 2002), pp. 2990-95.

[47] Central Hudson Gas & Electric Corp. v. Public Service Commission, 447 U.S. 557 (1980).

[48] 447 U.S. at 566.

[49] 533 U.S. 525 (2001).

[50] Id. at 561-66.

[51] The Massachusetts regulation prohibited outdoor advertising "in any location that is within a 1,000 foot radius of any public playground, playground area in a public park, elementary school or secondary school." 940 Code of Mass. Regs. § 21.04(5)(a).

[52] Lorillard, 533 U.S. at 562.

[53] Id. at 562, 564-65.

[54] Id. at 564.

[55] Id. at 557 ("The Attorney General relies in part on evidence gathered by the FDA...").

[56] Id. at 561 ("[W]e conclude that the regulations do not satisfy the fourth step of the Central Hudson analysis.").

[57] Id. at 562.

[58] Id.

[59] Id.

[60] Id. at 563-66.

[61] Id. at 563 ("The uniformly broad sweep of the geographical limitation demonstrates a lack of tailoring.").

[62] Id.

[63] Id.

[64] 61 Federal Register 44506.

[65] Id.

[66] Id.

[67] Id.

[68] Discount Tobacco City & Lottery v. U.S., 764 F.3d 509 (6th Cir. 2012).

[69] Id. at 544-548.

[70] Id. at 547.

[71] Id. at 548.

[72] Id. (internal quotation marks omitted).

[73] Id. quoting Lorillard, 533 U.S. at 571.

[74] Id.

[75] Id. at 541.

[76] Id. at 542.

[77] Id. at 542-543.

[78] Id. at 543-544.

[79] Commonwealth Brands, Inc. v. United States, 678 F. Supp. 2d 512, 536 (W.D. Ky. 2010).

[80] 21 U.S.C. § 387a-1.

[81] 447 U.S. at 566.

[82] 533 U.S. at 565-66.

[83] The language of the Tobacco Control Act provides only that the FDA "include such modifications, if any, that the Secretary determines are appropriate." 21 U.S.C. § 387a-1.

[84] Department of Health and Human Services, Food and Drug Administration, "Request for Comment on Implementation of the Family Smoking Prevention and Tobacco Control Act," 75 Federal Register 13241-13243, March 19, 2010.

[85] Id. at 13242.

[86] Beyer et al., supra n. 46.

INDEX

D

E

F

G

H

I

J

L

M